As you travel the many
paths of life

Remember

Angels will always
walk beside you

No matter the path
you may choose

Theresa
Ducchia

RECEIVE THEIR MESSAGES

Enlightened Series

T M ORECCHIA

BALBOA
PRESS

A DIVISION OF HAY HOUSE

Balboa Press books may be ordered through booksellers or by contacting:

Balboa Press
A Division of Hay House
1663 Liberty Drive
Bloomington, IN 47403
www.balboapress.com
1 (877) 407-4847

Because of the dynamic nature of the Internet, any web addresses or links contained in this book may have changed since publication and may no longer be valid. The views expressed in this work are solely those of the author and do not necessarily reflect the views of the publisher, and the publisher hereby disclaims any responsibility for them.

The author of this book does not dispense medical advice or prescribe the use of any technique as a form of treatment for physical, emotional, or medical problems without the advice of a physician, either directly or indirectly. The intent of the author is only to offer information of a general nature to help you in your quest for emotional and spiritual well-being. In the event you use any of the information in this book for yourself, which is your constitutional right, the author and the publisher assume no responsibility for your actions.

Any people depicted in stock imagery provided by Thinkstock are models, and such images are being used for illustrative purposes only.
Certain stock imagery © Thinkstock.

Print information available on the last page.

ISBN: 978-1-5043-4007-6 (sc)
ISBN: 978-1-5043-4009-0 (hc)
ISBN: 978-1-5043-4008-3 (e)

Library of Congress Control Number: 2015914288

Balboa Press rev. date: 9/25/2015

CONTENTS

ACKNOWLEDGEMENTS

THE ANGELS AND ARCHANGELS DID it again! This is their book and I want to thank all the angels who came to me with their stories. I feel it a privilege and an honor to have been chosen to receive and record their messages. All of the angels were easy to work with. They came through to my thoughts very clearly. Some were quite jovial at times and so it was a lot of fun putting the stories together. Thank you, dear Angels, for your many words of wisdom to help me start to understand the meaning of life here on earth.

Many, many thanks go to my nephew, Ron F Sill, for his artwork. Ron is a very talented artist and gave freely of his time to review the stories and suggest the details of a drawing reflective of a specific story. I enjoy working with Ron because he is open to my ideas as well as offering some very insightful suggestions regarding the artwork. Thank you, Ron. I appreciate your help and enjoy working with you.

I would also like to thank my sister, Cathie Ramone, for her help in reviewing and editing the manuscript. I warned her there was a lot of work involved, but she gladly said she wanted to be a part of the project. Thank you, Cathie, for all your time and expert editing advice.

Many, many thanks to my wonderful, loving husband, Michael, for his unending support, patience and understanding of the time I needed for this project. He was also a major part of my editing team and his reviews and comments were invaluable. I truly appreciate his support for this project from beginning to end. Thank you, Michael.

And lastly, I want to say thank you, God, for your love and for sending me your angels. I enjoy working with them and receiving their special messages that are from you.

DEDICATION

To my guardian angels, Daniel and Agnes, who have been walking with me since I first entered the earth plane. I know now when I look back on my life there were times when they must have been really hustling to get through to me. Yes, I turned away from them for a period in my life and now I know they never left me. Their dedication to me is beyond description.

I am so happy that I finally woke up to their encouraging words and support. They moved me through some bumpy roads in my life and brought me to where I am today. When they send me a feather whether I am playing golf, or pondering a difficult situation, I know they are close by and I just smile and whisper 'thank you'.

So, Daniel and Agnes, I dedicate this book to you in honor of your service to God.

INTRODUCTION

THERE ARE MANY REALMS OF angels working with God to guide all humans through their journey on earth. The angels work with each spirit before it incarnates to the earth plane preparing it for the life the spirit has chosen once it comes to earth. Each spirit chooses to pursue a particular life experience with the intent of moving closer to God. Angels review with the spirit all the obstacles it will confront and how to overcome them. Once the soul incarnates to earth, the angels who prepared it for the incarnation never leave the spirit. They constantly watch, monitor, send messages and even take on a human form when necessary to help the soul stay with the written plan. This is very important, because without their help and guidance, humans inevitably wander off course. As they wander away from their plan, they wander away from God.

I am Michael Archangel and I would like to say a few words. All the archangels and angels are closely associated with the earth realm. We are very proud of the souls incarnating to earth and the varied lifestyles they have chosen to experience. We know it is very difficult to experience life on earth because of the many distractions the earth has to offer. But, just look around and you will see the angels. We are very good at sending you signs and messages. Sometimes we are sooo blatant, yet a human will still not get it. We just look at each other, like you would look at someone, and say how can they be so blind? So, we try again, and again, and again to guide and protect the souls on earth. Life is not easy on earth, I know, but life does not have to be difficult either. Only you make it difficult for yourself by not opening your eyes and hearts to us angels. So, come, hold my hand and the hands of your guardian angels. Give us your troubles and your successes. It's time to start enjoying life. Stay with us, stay with God.

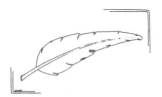

Kadziel

My name is Kadziel and I am with the angels of God. I want everyone to know there is a tremendous amount of love pouring down on the earth realm. However, many times God's love is returned unopened. This is so very, very sad. But many humans would say they are very, very sad also because of their life on earth. They are not happy; they seem to be on automatic pilot. Get up, go to work, meet friends, come home, watch TV and go to bed. They are in a rut, they would say. Their eyes are not open to the beauty of the world around them. What beauty, they would say. They are in a big city that is busy, dirty, crowded, and with lots of crime. Beauty is not there. And you might be saying to yourself that you do not identify with that description. You live in a small town, which is a little busy, and you have lots of friends. You see the trees change color in the fall and the flowers bloom in the spring. You say you believe you are happy. But I must report that love has been returned to us from both places.

Where there is happiness in the heart, there is God. Examine all that God has given you, all your talents, and your friends and family. Why, then, are you unhappy? If you believe your life is in a rut, talk to us about it if you want to escape your perceived rut. Some humans do not want to change. It takes energy and they are not willing to put forth that energy. They return God's love unopened to us. Many humans believe that if they make a specific request, a miracle will occur. And when it doesn't happen their way, they lose interest in us. A miracle will occur but often not in the way it is perceived it should be. When we angels receive a request for help, we respond immediately. We will send thoughts to the individual on when to leave a job or search for a transfer, or how to get out of a bad relationship. Being in a rut, many times, means that one is walking down the wrong path in life. When we receive the cry for help, we work feverishly to guide that individual to his written path.

Let me tell you the stories of two of my recent charges on the earth plane. The first is a lawyer who lived in a very large city and the second is of a young female artist who lived in a small town by the ocean.

The young man, who lived in the city, was very happy when he first arrived primarily because he left a small farming community. He thought that by moving away from the small town and moving to the big city that he had successfully escaped what he perceived as small town thinking. In the big city, he was now exposed to a broader base of thinking and opinions relative to both national and international events. He secured a prominent position in a well-established law firm and thought he was on top of the world. He couldn't wait until he returned home to boast of his monetary success and newfound worldly knowledge. He worked very hard for many months to learn the nuances of his position... the people in high positions that he should get close to, who to avoid, and above all how to play office politics. Without realizing his own time commitment to his position, the young lawyer was spending twelve to fourteen hours a day in this position. He did this for several years becoming totally wrapped up in the company. His weekends always included politicking with high-level lawyers and clients. With everything going on in his life, he never once asked us angels for any help or guidance. He was so busy working to succeed in life that he forgot what life was truly about. When he finally found time to go home, he dearly wanted to tell his family and friends all that he had learned in the big city and how successful he was. But the only thing he did was crash in his old bed in the family home and sleep for two days. His parents and siblings kept looking in on him to make sure he was okay. His mother cooked his favorite dinner and memories of past happiness filled him with every bite. His mother could see the sadness in his eyes and asked her son if he was truly happy with his success. He immediately shook his head yes, but lowered his eyes. She knew that he was not. She reminded him that when he was a child how he would look at the twinkling stars and say they were the angels winking at him. She asked if he looked at the stars in the big city. He said the city lights obscured the stars but he really wanted to say that he was usually too busy working. She reminded him that even though he could not see the stars very clearly, he could still talk to the angels. She asked if he remembered all the prayers he sent to the angels when he was a child. He said yes and now there was a twinkle in his eyes. He was starting to remember. He remembered as a child he always talked to his angels, in school, on the baseball field, and during a school test. Yes, he remembered the good feeling of having the angels with him back then. When did you grow away from the angels, his mother asked? He responded that he did not know, probably in college or the big city. He said he just didn't have time for them right now. His mother said that he needed the angels now more than he ever did before. Look at your life she told him, you just about exist. I bet you don't even know one of your neighbors. I don't have time, he exclaimed. Make time, she said. Your life is in a rut. Talk to the angels, they will tell you how to be successful and happy. You need to open up to them and you need to do it now.

The young lawyer thought about this conversation on his drive back to the city. His mother said look for the beauty where you live. He thought, there is no beauty; only dirty sidewalks, noisy streets, noisy kids, and panhandlers. No, there is no beauty where I live in the city.

The young man resumed his frantic lifestyle and then about three weeks later I heard him calling me. You see, I am his guardian angel. I was so happy to hear him calling me again. He told me he was in trouble, that he had seen some documents in the law firm that would incriminate three leading lawyers and possibly cause the large law firm to close. What should I do, the young lawyer asked as he glanced upward. I did not answer immediately, allowing the young lawyer time to regroup. He needed to grasp the entire picture of what he read, who was involved, and the part he must play in this scenario. He had to realize this could be the end of his successful career. And if he kept quiet, he would be a part of their dishonest scheme.

He walked home to his apartment that night and unconsciously looked up at the sky. He was surprised to see the stars. They were bright and twinkling just as he remembered as a child. Are you there, he whispered? Yes, yes, I am here. I have been waiting for you for a long time, I answered. I turned up the lights on the stars he was looking at. He noticed they seemed to get brighter. I believe you are here with me, he said aloud, continuing to stare at the twinkling stars. I then moved a star across the sky a little slower than usual to make sure it caught his eye. YES, he exclaimed! You truly are here. I was so happy to be back in touch with him that I was shouting to the angels in heaven. He's back, he's back, I shouted. The angels were elated for me. The young lawyer started talking about the troubling situation at his law firm. He was visibly upset as he poured his heart out to me. He kept saying over and over that I had helped him so many times in the past, and he hoped he would hear me again. He said he knew he had to make a decision by the end of the week since time was of the essence in stopping their illegal practices. He told me he was turning it all over to me to sort out and he welcomed my direction. He asked that I speak clearly so he wouldn't misinterpret my directions. He said he was very sad about this dilemma because he knew he would probably lose his job. With that all said, and with a very sad heart, he looked at the twinkling stars again. I wanted to reassure him I truly heard every word he said so I sent another star across the sky and sent him a feather that floated to his feet. He picked it up and whispered thank you.

I knew I had to come down to him for this situation. He usually worked late on Wednesday nights and would eat at a local pub. There were not many people there at this time of night so it would be easy to talk. I let him finish his dinner when I sauntered over to his table and asked if I could join him. He looked up, puzzled, and said sure, why not? I told him he looked very troubled and asked if he just wanted to talk. He looked at me like I was crazy. He said he had a lot on his mind but was not at liberty to discuss it. I looked him in the eyes and told him that nothing on earth could be that bad to make him look and feel so sad. He looked directly back at me, commented I had very kind eyes, and said yes, there truly are some very bad things happening around him. I changed my approach to small talk to try to calm him down. After he finally relaxed, I told him that humans come to earth with special assignments to complete before they return to the other side. He really thought I was crazy with that statement but he didn't back away. I continued on, saying he was probably confronting one of those assignments right now. He lowered his eyes and said softly 'I believe that I am'. I told him he could ignore the problem at work completely and pretend he didn't know anything and continue on with his busy life climbing the corporate lawyer ladder. He would probably be very successful and famous someday. But his knowledge of this corruption with his associates would always haunt him, especially as he saw other lives being destroyed. Yes, I repeated, this is probably a special assignment written in your life plan. You may or may not have the chance to complete this assignment in this lifetime if you choose not to act at this time. Remember, the tasks you established before you incarnated are all meant to further develop your soul to bring you closer to God. I stood to leave and the young man looked up sadly and said thanks. I told him if he wanted to talk again to just ask for Kadziel. As he got up to leave, the young lawyer noticed a feather resting on his shoe and knew he was talking to an angel.

I was now back in his life bringing him messages of God's love. He listened carefully to my message in the pub that night and exposed the fraudulent law firm. The other lawyers were proud that he stood up and exposed the illegal activities of the firm to the world. He gained strength and confidence from this life assignment. The remaining lawyers stayed together and opened their own law firm. The young lawyer was now thriving in an honest law business despite his earlier fears of being disgraced and unemployed.

He was now seeing God everywhere in the busy city. He smiled at everyone as he weaved his way through the crowded streets, noticing little pots of flowers outside many shops. Even the panhandlers didn't look so bad any more. He smiled at them and told them to talk to their angels. I was elated. Everyone over here was celebrating. We were able to help another soul experience God's messages; the messages of love that we bring to everyone. So, you see, life on the earth plane does not have to be difficult. Sure, you may have some tough times but with our help, you can achieve success in completing all of your earthly assignments.

Let me continue on about God's messages being returned unopened. When these messages of love are returned to us, we angels examine the reasons very carefully. Did we not speak loud enough, did we not send enough signs, what more could we have done to deliver our messages? I had a beautiful young woman whom I was directed to help through some very difficult tasks. She had several assignments to confront because she wanted to advance her soul as much and as fast as possible. She truly loved God and believed, with our help, she would be able to succeed in all her tasks.

She lived by the ocean and loved walking on the beach, talking to us and sharing all her recent experiences. She had successfully completed several of her predestined tasks. She remained in constant contact with us, knowing how we helped her traverse those paths. As we watched over her, we suddenly saw her life slowing down. She wasn't as cheerful as usual. She stopped communicating with us. She was going down a different path. I stayed by her side day and night whispering messages to her constantly. Nothing. She always heard me before. I sent her numerical signs, which I knew she could read immediately. Nothing. I sent her songs, feathers, and billboard messages. Nothing. What has happened? Why has she closed her heart to God? I needed to investigate more closely because this sudden change doesn't happen overnight. Something or someone was influencing her and moving her away from God.

I met her while walking on the beach. I approached from behind and said hello but she did not respond. I started to walk with her. She looked up and was startled that I was walking by her side. She looked very tired and disheveled and grumbled to leave her alone. Of course, I stayed with her. I mentioned that she used to love walking by the ocean and talking to the angels. What has happened, why did you change? Being slightly inebriated, she mumbled that God didn't like her any more. WHAT? How do you know that, I asked? Because I used to talk to Him and His angels all the time and I always received help and information when I needed it. Then I started to get sick. It got worse and worse with no one knowing what I had. I talked to the angels all the time but got nothing from them. Are you sure, I asked? Yes, I'm sure, she answered. Well, how about the time the angels sent you the article about early detection of breast cancer? That was just a flyer, she answered, and that was put on the front windows of all the cars in the parking lot. Maybe the angels were sending messages to a lot of other people who needed to be checked, I said. Why did you dismiss the breast cancer seminar that was held where you worked? The angels sent you that email information also. I didn't have time, she said, and besides I was in good health. There was no reason to sit through a seminar and become totally paranoid about the disease. Well, you know, knowledge about any disease is your first line of defense. So, you turned away from God because you have breast cancer, I asked? Yes, she said, wouldn't you? No, I think God would be my mainstay the moment I got the news. Hah, she exclaimed, easy for you to say, you are well and I am not.

We continued walking together for several more miles, bantering all the way. She would not give up the idea that God had deserted her. She believed that if God loved her and sent the angels to her, she would have a perfect life. I liked working with the angels, I really did, she said. I had fun interpreting their messages. But no more, I know now they are around me only in the good times. It's easier to see them when everything is lollipops and roses. No, she said, I guess I have to go through this alone. I asked her to look at it from another angle. Why do you think you developed cancer? There is no reason, she responded. I have lived a good, upstanding life, no drugs, no smoking, good relationships, and a successful career. I believe that I have been abandoned. Did you ever think about what you might learn from this experience, I asked? No, what is there to learn, how to tolerate pain, what scarves to wear for a baldhead, or how to graciously vomit my guts out? How can these be lessons, they are just different forms of torture. That's not very earth shattering to me, she said. And then there is the possibility that I will die just when my hair comes back. Or you may not, I quipped. Look at your life, I said, and all the experiences you have had and how much you have grown in your life and how you grew closer to God. Your world was opening to God and the angels and now everything is shut down. Please don't close your heart to God. You were given this task for a purpose, look beyond the physical, and look at the spiritual, look at the development of your soul. What you are saying is very heavy, she responded. I'm not sure I buy into it. I need time, but I don't believe your thinking will make its way into my persona. It is just too farfetched to wrap my head around. She said she was tired so we returned to her beach house. I told her that I would always be with her and to call me anytime. She asked for my phone number, but I told her to just say my name, Kadziel, and I would come. She just stared at me and turned to go into her house.

I stayed very close to this beautiful woman as she went through her cancer treatments. Yes, she did loose her hair. I sent her pictures of very pretty scarves that would look stunning as they framed her beautiful face. She was extremely sick after each chemo treatment but endured it to the end. She was constantly tired but always put on a happy face for her friends. Even though she believed she was going to die during the treatments, she never opened her heart to God. Her suffering was so intense that she truly believed God was punishing her. I stopped by her beach house one afternoon to offer her some comfort. She recognized me and remembered my name. I asked her why she hadn't called me? She said she just couldn't because she knew that I would talk to her about a loving and caring God. Yes, you're right, I said. You have experienced a lot of suffering and God has been watching you very closely. He wants you to succeed with this experience. Her eyes widened. SUCCEED?? Succeed at what, she asked. You have to go inwards and examine your soul for what is written in your life plan for that answer, I said. No matter what is written, she answered, how can a caring and loving God be so cruel and let me suffer like this? You know, I said, you aren't the only person experiencing breast cancer and you won't be the last. I know, I know, she said, but I still ask you how can a caring and loving God let all these people suffer as we do with breast cancer? He is watching the development of their souls through this experience, I responded. You see, a soul has to be very strong to write cancer into its program before coming to the earth plane. You are only looking at what is happening to the body. The true healing process is found in the soul. So what if I die when this is over, she asked? So what if you do, I responded. Then all this was for nothing, she said. That is where you are wrong, I answered. It is through this suffering that the soul can open and move closer to God. Again, this is all about soul development and getting to know God at a higher level. Kadziel, she exclaimed, this is enough!! I am tired and all this talk about loving God when I am suffering so much is making me even angrier with God. She then asked how I knew so much about God and souls. I looked at her with tears in my eyes and told her that I was her guardian angel. She just shook her head and walked into the bedroom.

The young woman survived her cancer. She was more beautiful than before and was admired by many for enduring the treatments as well as she did. Unfortunately, she never called for me or even an archangel as she progressed through life, which presented her with several more obstacles to traverse. I sent her many signs to remind her I was always near to deliver God's messages, and to help her walk through life. All of our messages were returned unopened. I am very sad that this young woman is missing God's love and help but I won't give up and neither will God.

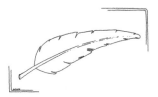

MALYON

I AM ARCHANGEL MALYON. I am not known on the earth plane but I am called upon by many guardian angels when they need assistance. Working with guardian angels is very rewarding. I can see first hand how very hard they work at assisting souls through many lifetimes on the earth plane. Guardian angels go to great lengths to guide and protect their assigned spirits and never hesitate to call on the archangels for extra help. The gift of free will makes it easy for souls to stray from their life plan. Now, if we could keep a soul on his chosen plan, his life would be joyous even when tragedy and suffering are written into that plan. Let me tell you about Telithe, the guardian angel to a very strong, determined young man.

Telithe was very excited to receive this young man as her earthly charge. Telithe knew from the beginning this soul had a strong personality and wanted to help him accomplish the goals he had written in his life plan. As a child, the young man was challenging to Telithe but she didn't miss a beat to protect and guide him. His parents taught him about God and the angels but he did not really care about them. His parents struggled to keep him in school and out of trouble and were very happy when he graduated from high school. He did not want to go to college at that time and announced he wanted to explore the world. Both parents were saddened by this decision because they knew he would be moving away from them. They felt that if they were nearby they could protect him from the many decisions he would make that would ultimately get him into trouble. He was a good boy but very strong willed and determined to make his own decisions in life. He was not open to advice from anyone. He wanted to experience life on his own terms. His parents knew the only thing they could do was to ask God to place as many angels around him as possible while he 'searched the world for excitement', as he would say. They knew he was really searching for himself.

Telithe had her hands full from the moment the young man left his hometown and headed for another country. He had a fair amount of money that he had saved and believed he could exist without a job for about a year. Upon arriving in the new country, he was very excited knowing he had so many new adventures to explore and no one to tell him 'no'. Telithe was right there with him guiding him to reputable parts of the new city and showing him signs where he could get a room. He looked around and decided he would be spending too much money and headed for a less expensive section of town. He thought a particular area of town looked okay and that he would be safe. He found a room that was small but clean. He started to notice that no one talked to him. Many looked at him with sinister eyes. They made him feel like he didn't belong there; they didn't want him there. Well, he thought, all the better. This will be a great challenge for me. I want to fit in just like a native, he told himself. He was able to speak the language of the country so he thought it was just a matter of time until he walked the neighborhood as if he grew up there. However, he did not have the local dialect and was easily recognized as an outsider.

Telithe was working feverishly watching over every decision the young man made. She knew he had chosen an area replete with drug lords, turf gangs, high stake gamblers, and professional panhandlers. A new face in this neighborhood was noticed immediately and all of these unsavory groups were on high alert. The young man was definitely unseasoned and ripe for the pickings. Which group would make the first move to either move him out of the neighborhood against his will or recruit him? Telithe sent him many thoughts to 'be aware', 'cross the street', 'look behind – watch your back'. Sometimes he received these thought messages but mostly he ignored them. He was determined to do everything his own way. He had not talked to his guardian angel, Telithe, since he was a little boy and then only under the guidance of his mother. Even then, he did not want anyone's help in his life, not even an angel.

One late afternoon, he stopped at a nearby pub for a beer and some conversation. As he walked through the door, everyone at the bar stopped their conversations and stared at him. He ignored their stares and sauntered to an empty booth. He was not afraid because he just felt he was the 'new kid on the block'. Telithe was very aware. She saw the imminent danger he was in. The group at the bar started talking again but the conversation was not about their business but about the kid in the booth. They believed him to be an undercover agent. They needed to investigate. Telithe sent many messages/warnings to the young man but they fell on deaf ears. He smiled when one of the drug lords came over to his table. He thought that now he was starting to make progress with the locals. The drug lord made light conversation, asking him where he was from and what business he had in the neighborhood. The young man picked up the demeanor of the older man and just shrugged his shoulders and said he had no immediate business; he was just experiencing the neighborhood. Looking at the drug lord, Telithe knew this could be the beginning of the end for the young man. Telithe called on some other angels to help protect this young man from possible injury. He had no idea who he was dealing with. Telithe then assumed human form and walked through the door of the pub. Again the men at the bar stopped and stared. She sauntered over to the young man and asked if she could join him. The drug lord leered at her, got up and returned to the bar. Who are you, the young man innocently asked? Just a friendly neighbor, she replied. She engaged him in light conversation and asked him to walk her home. She said she was sometimes afraid in this neighborhood. He looked puzzled. He replied he felt very comfortable living there. As they walked out, Telithe knew they would be followed. They walked many blocks while she explained the dangers in the area. She told him they were being followed but every time he turned around he saw no one. He decided not to believe her and thought she came in just to use him to her advantage for the night. He quickly said goodnight and turned away.

Days turned into months as the young man went to work for the drug lord he met at the pub. He knew the man was dealing drugs but felt he was safe from the law in this neighborhood. He was starting to see some of the elements Telithe described that evening many weeks before. He felt relatively safe now that he was in their business. He decided not to use any of the drugs he handled because he believed he could make more money by being sober. This was a red flag to the drug lords in the area. They let him continue doing small drug runs for them and then decided to bring him inside to get a better look at him. Telithe entered his life again to warn him. This was the only way she could communicate with him. She called out to him on the streets one night appearing to be slightly intoxicated. From her ruffled clothes he could not tell if she was a male or female. She looked him in the eyes and said she heard he was moving up in the business. He just stared at her. The word is on the street, she said. She commented that this could be really good or really bad for him. You know they are testing you, she said. Testing? Testing for what, he responded? To see who you are and who you are connected with. I don't understand, he said. I am just me. I make my own decisions, I live my own life and I am not connected to anyone. They don't know that, she said. Telithe looked at him for several seconds and said, 'watch your back, they are looking to kill you'. Again, he immediately rejected her advice and walked away.

The young man was feeling very confident now that he was given more responsibility. He joined many of the other guys at the local pub several nights a week. He was getting into a routine of learning the business by day and sometimes at night. He learned who to trust and how to spot an informer. He thought many times of the street person warning him that these people were going to kill him. I made the right decision to move on in this business, he concluded. I am making a lot of money and have made a lot of friends. Unknowingly, he was still being watched.

Telithe entered his life many times in the human form. She always assumed different human forms because he would reject her if she came to him in a previous form that he recognized. He would remember her advice and walk away before she could deliver her warning. Her messages were still the same, warning him of extreme danger. He was getting frustrated and tired of hearing this type of information from people on the street. He refused to believe he was in danger because he never saw any violence with his work group. They just moved drugs. He was now very comfortable walking the streets in this neighborhood in the early morning hours. Late one evening after completing his drug deliveries, monetary collections and working with new contacts to expand his territory, he headed back to his room slightly intoxicated but very satisfied. He liked his new life. The bosses listened to his ideas; he felt he was making his own decisions, living his life as he wanted. Suddenly there appeared in front of him two very large men who blocked his path. He tried to pass on the left, then the right, but they blocked the way. What do you want, he asked? He did not recognize them. They answered, 'you'. With that, they forcefully maneuvered him into a car and sped away. Talithe immediately came to me for my assistance. We both watched what was happening and knew their thoughts. The men were instructed to kill the young man. They took him to a deserted part of the city and pulled him from the car. He pleaded with them to tell him what they wanted from him.

They told him to be quiet but then, he recognized their voices. They were the guys he had seen in the pub several times talking to his bosses. He would nod to them in a friendly gesture never thinking that violence was part of this organization. He should have known though. Where there are drugs, there is crime and that crime can be violent. He saw it in the movies as a teen but always recognized when a wrong decision was made by one of the characters in the movies. He believed he was smarter than that. He believed he knew how to recognize elements that could harm him. He prided himself with his decisions. How did this happen, he thought. He feverishly searched his memory for signs that he missed. He saw them in the movies, why didn't he see them here? He had plenty of time to observe his environment. He had been in this neighborhood for over six months. He started to recall the warnings from the street people in the neighborhood. But what do they know, he asked himself? He never liked advice anyway. But, he thought, they all had the same message, even the streetwalker who asked to walk with him one night shortly after he arrived. What have I done, he cried to himself, what have I done?

After the men pulled the young man from the car they started to push him around abusing him verbally and physically. The young man was in no position to defend himself, but he tried very hard. After a short while, he was on the ground and barely conscious when he saw what appeared to be a gun in each of their hands. This is when Talithe and I appeared in human form. I was larger in stature than these men and so was Talithe. Two other angels accompanied us in the form of very large dogs. I told the men in a very loud and strong voice to step away and drop their weapons. They turned quickly around towards us and were ready to engage battle but we blinded them with bright light. They remained frozen in place. I kept the bright light strong in their eyes and again spoke sternly to them. I then lifted the light enough for them to see our figures. The guns fell from their hands as they stared in disbelief of our presence. They turned and ran.

The young man was severely beaten but still alive. Talithe had already alerted the authorities of violence in this area. We heard the sirens in the distance and stayed with the young man until they arrived. He would survive but his road to recovery was going to be long and hard.

When he was strong enough to leave the hospital in this foreign country, he returned to his hometown. He called his parents for the first time since leaving home and asked if he could come home again. His parents were ecstatic but stared in disbelief when they saw him. His swollen face and his body were covered with bruises; he used crutches to walk, and he wore an eye patch. After he settled into his old bedroom, he asked his parents to please let him be by himself. They respected his wishes and knew they had to wait patiently until he would tell them his story. His mother quietly thanked the angels for returning her son alive.

The young man attended physical therapy three days per week. Shortly after he started, he met a little girl who smiled each time she saw him and always said hello. She reminds me of a little angel, he told the therapist. Do you believe in angels, the therapist asked? I know about them, but no, I really don't believe in them. I don't understand how something we can't see or hear is going to help us. What's in it for them, he asked? The therapist responded, saying the angels bring us God's messages so it is really God who is watching us. The angels are happy when we receive their messages because they know this makes God happy. It still doesn't make sense to me, he answered. Look at your life right now, she said. I know the angels worked very hard sending you messages, trying to tell you of the danger you were in. Obviously, you didn't listen. The young man became very quiet as he thought of the street people who brought him warnings during his time in the foreign country. Were they angels, he thought? No, they were humans who just knew the ways of the neighborhood, he decided.

After two months, the young man was finally ready to talk with his parents about his life in the foreign country. He told them how he felt he was truly free being on his own and being able to converse in the native tongue. He cautiously told them of the neighborhood he selected and how he trusted everyone, from the drug lords to the panhandlers. His mother had tears in her eyes as she asked if he remembered the angels especially when the people he was working with turned against him. He said no. She told him they were there especially since he came out alive. This triggered his mind to remember the blinding light the night he was beaten and almost killed. He relayed this memory to his parents. They both started to cry as his mother told him that he was surrounded and protected by some powerful angels. She said that he probably had a few archangels there as well. He knew then that there was a higher source of power present on that fateful night.

The following week, he met the little girl again at physical therapy. She smiled angelically and said hello. Suddenly, he believed she was truly an angel. Her mother walked up to him and said hello in a foreign language. She asked him how he was progressing. He knew the language and recognized her voice. He asked if she was in her country lately and she said yes. She said she remembered seeing him in a pub shortly after he arrived. He squinted his eyes looking at her, trying to remember. I walked you to your home that night, he said. Yes, that's correct, she responded. Who are you, why are you here? My name is Talithe, she said. I am your guardian angel. He stared at her for what seemed an eternity. He blinked a few times and asked if she knew any of the street people in that neighborhood. She answered yes. He said he received several warnings from them telling him to leave the neighborhood. She shook her head and said, 'I know'. He then realized she was one of the street people disguised to bring him the messages. With his eyes wide open, he asked if she helped save him from his attackers. The blinding light, he said, was that you? She laughed and said she had some help from Archangel Malyon and several other angels. He took a deep breath and said thank you. I am so very sorry for dismissing you when you were in human form. I had no idea the power of angels and archangels.

The young man continued with his physical therapy for several more months. He progressed exceptionally well and recovered with not only a new body but also a new spirit. During this time he thought a lot about his life. He thought about how stubborn he was to have his own way even at the expense of others, and how naïve he was to always ignore helpful advice. He realized he was a very difficult person to be around even in his early childhood. I am a lucky person, he said to himself one day. I am lucky to be alive.

Before he ventured out again into the world in search of a new life, he asked his mother for advice to change his life. She quietly answered, 'talk to your guardian angel'. She reminded him of his experience meeting his angel and even knowing her name. She asked if he ever talked to her since he had been home. He said no, he hadn't thought of doing that. He said he thought Talithe was there only to warn him of danger and he would now pay attention. He asked, 'what can she do for me now'? 'O My Goodness', his mother exclaimed. Talithe can do a lot for you. She will open doors of opportunity to direct you back to your written life plan. Once you are on your recorded plan, which you wrote in heaven before you incarnated, your life will be full of love and happiness. This does not mean to say your life will be free of difficulties but with Talithe's help, you will be able to handle those difficulties with ease. She will send you many signs to help you. You must learn to understand every message that comes from Talithe. The young man sat with his mother and thoughtfully asked how he should start. He felt overwhelmed with all this information. His mother advised him to first open his heart to God. Look around and see God in the landscape, on the busy streets, the little children, the crippled man trying to help another walk across the street. God is all around you, look for Him, recognize Him, say hello to Him. Also every morning, say hello to Talithe and welcome her into your life. Talk to her throughout the day. I know she is very happy now since you have decided to change your life. Do all this and doors of opportunity will open to you. You must keep your mind open to recognize Talithe's signs. You will receive her messages in your heart. If you think you have received a sign/message to apply for a specific job, contact the employer. If this message was from Talithe, the entry process will be very easy and smooth. If it was an idea you came up with and tried to interpret it as being from Talithe, you will meet with delays and roadblocks. Walk away from this idea and know that it was not meant to be.

I watched in admiration how Talithe guided the young man, as he grew stronger in his knowledge and love for God and the angels. She talked to him every day even though he couldn't hear her in the beginning because he did not yet understand how to listen to his heart to hear her messages. She sent him very simple messages in the beginning. He learned quickly to see her signs…repeating numbers, messages on billboards. She especially liked to send him messages through his Ipod. He responded to them immediately. Talithe was very happy with his progress.

As a very successful lawyer, the young man chose to help those who got caught in the web of drugs. He remembered how Talithe and I saved his life. He would walk the streets extending a helping hand to those who would receive him. He especially tried to help those caught selling illegal drugs. His interest wasn't necessarily legal assistance but spiritual assistance. He befriended many drug dealers who came to know his past. He slowly introduced them to the angels. Many were skeptical and said he was hallucinating. He believed if he could save one soul from the near-death experience he had when selling drugs, he would be happy.

Talithe came to me when the young man was ready to return to us. She was very happy with the results of his life. As the young man approached, he looked at me and then at Talithe. I remember you both, he said. You saved my life. You gave me a second chance on earth. Yes, we replied. Thank you; thank you with all my heart. We then escorted him to God who was smiling down on him as He came to greet us.

ARYANE AND PHEBIONES

My name is Aryane and I work many times with Phebiones. We are archangels who are assigned to souls who have decided to return to the earth plane against the advice of the great Masters. Yes, souls on this side can still exert free will. When a soul returns to us after completing a life experience on earth, there is a system whereby the soul rests for awhile. It then begins the process of evaluating its experiences from its immediate past life on the earth plane. The experiences and resulting learning processes are evaluated by the soul to determine if the soul accomplished the goals that were written in its life plan. If the soul did not achieve success with its life's experiences, the soul will discuss the event(s) with one or more of the Masters. The soul must then restore its energy before attempting to write a new plan, under the guidance of a Master. The Master watches over the progress of the soul on this side and decides when that soul is ready to reincarnate. The soul always has the option to remain here or return to the earth plane.

Many souls have incarnated to earth against the advice of the Masters. Souls are strongly advised not to ignore this advice but they may choose to exercise free will with the belief they are strong enough to accomplish what they failed to do in their previous life on earth. These souls are advised that their new life may be very difficult because their soul is not rested or it is not strong enough to work on the earth plane. Phebiones and I befriend these souls before they incarnate and try to incorporate into their being that we archangels are with them every step of the way along with their guardian angels. We know this knowledge will be lost once the separation veil is dropped after several years on earth. Many times, however, a soul will reach deep into its heart and start to remember our words.

Phebiones and I walked with the guardian angel of a male spirit who made a decision to return to the earth plane before he completed his review and restoration time with us. Even over here, he was anxious. He wanted to complete his learning tasks as quickly as possible. He always wanted to move on, move ahead fast. We knew he would be a great challenge with this early return to earth.

As a baby, he was never content. His parents had two other children who were very calm and happy but were frustrated with their new little boy. He became progressively worse as a toddler. He just could not calm down. He had difficulty learning basic skills at his young age. His guardian angel, Larnya, stayed very close to protect him from harmful situations. His parents realized, when he was 4 years old, he was not developing as he should. He angered easily; he fought verbally and physically with his siblings. The medical doctors diagnosed him as just hyperactive. They said he would grow out of it eventually. They offered medications, but the parents resisted, not wanting to pump drugs into their child.

Suddenly at six years old, the young boy suddenly became quiet and still. He would sit for long periods of time just staring. He made very little contact with his brother and sister. He didn't seem to know who they were. Larnya was there constantly. She talked to him and he responded. She told him she was there to help him. She asked if he remembered his archangels, Aryane and Phebiones. He said no. Larnya stayed with him, consoling his soul. His parents, alarmed at this sudden change in behavior, took him to medical experts. They did a variety of tests and told the parents their child was autistic. They immediately felt guilty believing they may somehow be the cause.

The boy continued in this withdrawn state for many years. He received special developmental education in an attempt to mainstream him into the local high school. His progress was slow. Larnya never left his side, talking with him, trying to help him acknowledge his reason for withdrawing. Phebiones and I worked with Larnya knowing the soul was overwhelmed on the earth plane. He didn't know how to handle life and the older he got, the more difficult life became. He just wanted to escape the challenges he wrote in his life's plan so he decided to withdraw completely. He told us he felt safe there. He wanted to complete his time on earth in this state.

Our job now was to help him reach deep into his memory to remember our counseling before he incarnated. Sometimes he would hear us but mostly he would not. Eventually, Larnya's messages were beginning to be received. He recognized feelings of love she would send to him with the message to open his heart to God. She also kept repeating our names to him. One day, he said our names aloud. His parents and teachers were puzzled. What was he saying? Is he speaking another language? Phebiones and I were also sending messages of love from God daily. When he spoke our names, we knew his subconscious was opening. We spoke louder and in harmony with Larnya. We wouldn't give up. He came to us one night while he slept. We reminded him of our warnings about how difficult life would be for him since he chose to return before he was fully prepared. He acknowledged remembering and asked what he should do now that he was on the earth plane. We reviewed our plan to guide and protect him but told him that he must remember to call on us, to let us into his heart and not try to accomplish his challenges on his own. We asked him to remember this meeting and that we would help him walk out of his sleep on earth to become a functioning human.

At the age of 18, the young man seemed to open his eyes and walk out of his dream world. Because he remembered the dream of when he visited us, he called on Larnya, Phebiones and I every day. We showered him with God's love and sent him many signs and messages to help him in his new life. He stepped into life slowly and carefully because he was still frightened of life. His family and friends were elated and somehow knew not to overwhelm or crowd him. His parents and the medical profession had no idea how this happened and searched for medical explanations. There were none.

As the young man grew stronger mentally, his hyper personality began to disappear. He developed a daily ritual of talking to Laryna and the archangels, asking them for protection and guidance every day. He felt a calmness starting to envelop his personality. He wasn't sure why this was happening but with this calmness his eyes were opening to the beauty around him. He saw those who needed help and those who helped others. His anger subsided significantly and he became aware of many strangers approaching him, smiling at him, and saying hello. The young man felt in his heart he needed to reach out to help those less fortunate than he. He became an advocate of autism. He did not understand how he was able to move off the autism spectrum but believed he could somehow help others, be it family, friends, teachers, or medical personnel, by relating his experience. He started talking to small groups. He told of his life experience including his experiences with angels and how he would feel an overwhelming swell of love surrounding him when he was sitting alone at home. He stated how he kept remembering these strange names but couldn't pronounce them. With all these strange feelings, he said, he remembered not being afraid. The word angel kept coming to him, he related, but at that point he had no idea what the word 'angel' meant. He stayed with these thoughts because they made him feel good. He related how one day his mother overheard him say the word 'angel' several times. Upon hearing this, he said, she taught me to say 'hello guardian angel' daily. He stated he believed this was the beginning of his return from his dark, lonely world. He said that the angels bring us God's love and with His love and messages, we are able to move through the challenges life presents to us.

The young man excelled in his work to bring the angels and God's love to those who would hear him. He felt very fulfilled when he presented his life's experience and the role of the angels to those groups involved with autism. He believed if he could educate the family and friends of autistic children to help them reach inside themselves and feel the angels surrounding them, he would be fulfilling his life's purpose.

The young man truly exceeded his goal to educate thousands regarding the power of angels. As he crossed over to the other side, Laryna, his guardian angel, met him with open arms. She was so proud he was able to overcome the challenges of returning to the earth too soon after his previous life. She also noticed a change in his soul's personality. He was a lot calmer now, happy to be at this new level of soul development. Phebiones and I greeted him next. He smiled when he saw us and said, 'thank you for being patient and not giving up on me'. He said he knew it was difficult for us because he was so head strong and now he understands the need for souls to prepare and grow strong before returning to earth. We escorted him to the Masters who very proudly related that he accomplished his life's challenge for this incarnation. The Masters then stepped aside for God who smiled at the young man and said, 'welcome home'.

PHEBIUS

LET ME INTRODUCE MYSELF. My name is Phebius Archangel. I am with the archangel fleet that cares for children. Many times a spirit will choose to incarnate to the earth plane for a short period of time. We help prepare that spirit to experience what is necessary to assist with its soul development. Many times this spirit chooses to return to the earth plane at this level to help another spirit with soul development. Still other souls return to help scientists understand a complex disease. We archangels find it commendable of these spirits for their generosity in helping each other advance their souls by returning to the earth plane to be a part of unlocking the mysteries of life on earth.

One particular spirit was anxious to return to the earth plane. The spirit chose to take on a three-fold task attempting to complete all three goals in a short time period. We worked with the spirit to prepare it for its return to earth. The spirit knew it would be able to communicate with us for a period of time before the veil dropped that would prevent us from communicating easily. We re-assured the spirit we would be with it constantly. The great Masters and we angels reviewed the work plan. The time arrived for the spirit to incarnate to earth.

The excited and nervous parents received their little boy with much happiness and love. The child was perfect in every way. He was healthy, alert and beautiful. The child's entire family was present for his birth. It was a great occasion for this family.

The baby's grandparents were worried for their children when they got married. They felt they were not prepared because they were young, and of different cultures. There was much dissension in both families because of this union. This family conflict just made the child's parents even more determined to prove their parents wrong. They loved each other very much and believed their love was strong enough to weather all the turmoil they would experience in their marriage. And turmoil there was. The families would not interact with each other on any level. Their dislike for each other rose to a feeling of hatred. The children tried to bring peace to the families but eventually they were ignored. Each family member seemed to thrive on verbally attacking the other family in the presence of the child's parents. This hurt them deeply and they relied on their love for each other to survive family events.

The young couple was married for several years before their little boy was born. In that time, the fighting between the families continued with it creeping into the couple's relationship. They had small squabbles; they criticized each other and they were slow to say they were sorry. The little boy's mother became aware of their deteriorating relationship when a close friend asked her if she and her husband were considering a divorce. The mother looked at her friend with wide eyes and a shocked look on her face. She asked her friend why she asked this. She asked if there was something she should know. She immediately thought her husband was maybe having an affair. The friend responded that every time she was with the couple they always seemed to fight. She told the mother their criticisms had intensified so much she was uncomfortable when they were all together. The mother thanked her friend for her observations and comments and assured her there were no divorce proceedings planned.

The young couple regrouped and visited a marriage counselor who showed them how the outside family fighting was impacting their lives. He showed them how to awaken their love for each other and how to protect themselves from the outside interferences. The young couple visited the counselor several times and worked very hard to reignite their love. It was returning slowly because both sides of the family saw the couple come close together again so they tried even harder to break them apart. The counselor warned them that their renewed love would probably spark stronger family attacks against them. The couple prevailed with their mission to rise above the fighting and hatred in their families. They were even stronger now and were determined to survive and show their families that all cultures can co-exist. Hatred must be replaced with love, they consistently said to their families.

Total love surrounded the little boy the moment he was born. His parents were bursting with joy and happiness. In the hospital room, they both noticed the families were talking to each other exclaiming how beautiful the child was. They were all cooing over his little fingers and toes. It was a great moment to experience the parents later said to each other. The child seemed to bring peace to the families. They all united to celebrate with the little boy. He was the 'apple' of each of the grandparents' eyes. Both families eagerly volunteered to watch the little boy when his mother returned to work. Then jealousy set in. One family felt they were being slighted if the baby was at the other family's house more than theirs. Then the bickering began. Each family believed they cared for the baby better than the other family. The fighting between the families resumed shortly after. The parents were sad because they believed the child showed the families they could truly co-exist.

The families returned to their hateful fighting. The parents worked to reduce their visits to both families due to this unsettled environment. They refused to expose their little boy to the arguments and constant negative energy. They protected their little boy as much as possible and worked to surround him with total love and happiness. He was their life now. Their families would just have to figure out on their own how to stop fighting and find love. The young family enjoyed their special moments together.

The little boy excelled in learning to walk and talk at an early age. He giggled and laughed as he played with his toys. He was a pleasure to be around. On one of his routine doctor's visits, the young mother was asked if the little boy had fallen or bumped into anything sharp. She readily answered no. The mother stated she had not seen any bruises or bumps on the child. The doctor placed the mother's hand on the child's back and helped her trace a small area on one side. She was puzzled and told the doctor she did not feel anything. He helped her press a little harder and then she felt two round knots. The doctor assured her the lumps may be nothing but he wanted to investigate further. She readily agreed.

When the tests were complete, the doctor informed the parents the child had a very rare form of cancer. Research scientists were just beginning to study this type of cancer, he said. I suggest you take him to a children's hospital where there are doctors and medical professionals with knowledge of and experience with this type of cancer. The parents cried and held each other for a very long time before they left the doctor's office.

The child was admitted to the children's hospital to undergo another barrage of tests. The families were now informed of the news. Both families were unusually quiet. Fingers were pointing and each family blamed the other for carrying the cancer gene. The child's parents now had enough of this fighting and hatred and forbid any verbal assaults in their presence and in the presence of their child. The child's mother stated in a very strong voice the negative energy emanating from their hatred has the power to interfere with the child's healing process.

The little boy made many friends in the hospital. He was a happy soul and even though many of the tests were intense and long, he tolerated them well. His parents believed their child somehow knew he was there to help the doctors. One afternoon, his mother entered the room quietly and heard her son talking. She looked around and saw no one. He is just talking to his imaginary friend, she thought. He seemed to be talking a lot more lately to this friend. She tried to listen as she tiptoed closer to his bed. She heard him say 'yes' and 'thank you' many times. When her little boy turned his head and saw her standing there, he smiled a radiant smile. He looks like an angel, she thought. She asked him to whom was he talking. He looked puzzled at this question and told her it was his friend, Phebius. He told her that Phebius was there many times when she was there so why didn't she ever say hello to him? She apologized to her son for not saying hello to his friend but explained she could not really see Phebius. He looked at her not understanding why she could not see his friend. He is here all the time, the little boy exclaimed. The mother humored her little boy with his vivid imagination. He was only four years old.

The child endured many tests before the doctors gave their prognosis. The child's parents met with several doctors and researchers one afternoon about two months after the child entered the hospital. They described in great detail all they had learned from studying their son's cancer. It is extremely rare, one doctor commented, this is the fourth case we have seen in two years. We need to understand it as much as possible, the doctors and researchers stated, because we believe this cancer will be occurring more in the near future. Unfortunately, we have no treatments at this time to help your little boy. The information we were able to gather from studying him is invaluable, the team related to the parents. There is now enough data on this cancer to help the researchers decide how to treat the disease with medication.

The parents left the hospital together and walked for several hours in a nearby park. Shocked and with a heavy heart, they kept asking themselves 'why'. Why their child? Why us? What did we do to deserve this? Maybe we shouldn't have married, they said, maybe our parents were right. Doubt and fear were making their way into their lives. We still love each other, they said, so why do we doubt our love? They were very confused and anxious with all that was happening to their son. They knew he would return to God soon even though the doctors did not give them a time frame. They walked and walked, hand in hand, trying to make sense of the information they were just given and how to tell their families. And what about their son, they said to each other. Should he know he would be returning to God? With tears in their eyes, they looked at each other and said they needed help, preferably from God.

They returned to their son's room and heard him talking as they entered the room. They listened in on his conversation with Phebius. He asked if he would see God again and they saw him smile. At that point, the parents realized his imaginary friend was an angel. They let him continue talking a few more minutes and he suddenly turned when he heard his mother say 'hello Phebius'. The little boy's face lit-up as he believed his mother could see Phebius. He told his parents what he was talking about with his friend. He said Phebius told him he would be in the hospital for a little while longer and then he was going to travel to see God. He said he told Phebius he was both happy and sad. He said he was happy because he remembers all the beautiful angels where God lives. He asked his mother if she would be with him and the angels and God. Holding back the tears in her eyes, she shook her head no. She told her little boy he was very special and God missed him in heaven. Why am I special, he asked. She and her husband sat on the bed with their son and lovingly explained he had a special mission on earth. The little boy beamed with joy. I am special, he reiterated. They then told him how he helped the cancer doctors and researchers understand the type of cancer he has and now they can go to work to get medicine for other children who get the same cancer. The little boy threw his shoulders back and smiled the biggest smile they had ever seen. He was very proud to know God sent him on this special mission to help other children.

The little boy spent the following months walking around the hospital, smiling at the other sick children, and telling them he had a special mission from God. He wanted the other children to talk to their angels about their special missions. The little boy filled the children's rooms with happiness and love. He made everyone feel good including the doctors, nurses and attendants. Word quickly spread throughout this children's hospital about a little boy spreading joy to all its cancer patients. He was getting weaker now but his enthusiasm never waned. The news media heard of the good work this special little boy was doing at the hospital and asked to interview him. He was beside himself with joy. He was very relaxed and uninhibited with the questions from the news people. He stated very strongly he was on a special mission from God with his type of cancer. He even asked one of the interviewers if she talked to her angels and did she have a special mission also.

As the child grew weaker, he asked if he could go home for a while. He missed his dog and his bedroom with all his toys and special gifts from his parents and grandparents. The doctors approved the discharge and walked him to the hospital entrance with tears in their eyes. Many thanked the little boy for all his help and for all the love and joy he brought to the hospital. Before he climbed into the car, he turned around to the hospital and saw many of his friends standing at their windows and waving goodbye. He waved and sat next to his mother and father as his grandfathers sat in the front seat.

There was great jubilation here in heaven when the little boy's guardian angels escorted him to me. 'Phebius, I'm back' he exclaimed, as he ran toward me. I put my arms out to receive the young soul. He immediately asked how he did. I took him by the hand as we walked toward his parents' house. He watched and listened as they talked in awe about how heroic their little boy was. They emphasized if one little boy could bring that much love and joy into the world in such a short time, it was time the families learn from their son and bring love and joy into their own lives as well as others. He then saw many tears and apologies between the families and the promise to keep the love of their hero alive in their hearts and actions. I then walked him to the children's hospital to let him see how many of the children had made contact with their angels and how the children were helping their parents understand how important it was for them to experience cancer.

So Phebius told the little soul he was very successful. You had three major accomplishments, she said: first, you contributed to the understanding of a little known but very virulent cancer; second, you united two families of different cultures with a hatred for each other that dated back hundreds of years; and third, you brought joy, hope and happiness to a hospital filled with pain and sadness.

As we returned to the angels, a great light descended on us. The little soul was frightened when he saw the light and all the angels. He hesitated but then ran to God as He walked in. God picked up the little soul and hugged him dearly and showered him with love. He smiled at the little soul and welcomed him home.

Rashiel

I WOULD LIKE TO INTRODUCE myself. I am Angel Rashiel. Together with the guardian angels, I help those spirits who have elected to return to the earth plane to experience life with a handicap. I and many other angels in my realm prepare these spirits for the many difficulties they will face on earth. Some souls may choose a particular hardship in an effort to advance their souls more quickly toward God. Others may choose to return with this hardship because they failed a previous task on earth. When a task that is written in a soul's Akashic record is not completed in a lifetime, the soul chooses how to complete that task in another visit to the earth plane. This requires a lot of preparation before a soul incarnates so we review every detail of the chosen hardship with the soul and the soul's guardian angels. We show the soul the physical as well as the spiritual difficulties it will encounter and what it must accomplish in this period for success in completing this selected life task.

Let me tell you of two souls that I assisted recently. Both were very experienced souls when they chose to return to the earth plane with selected handicaps. The angels who worked with me to prepare these souls for this experience believed both souls were strong enough to endure the difficulties and accomplish their soul's written tasks. Both wanted very strongly to accomplish their difficult tasks to move closer to God. We reviewed extensively all the facets of their tasks, what needed to be done, how to overcome all the obstacles they would encounter by identifying them, discussing how to confront them and then continue on with their lives. We emphasized the 'continuing on' part because this is very difficult to do. We taught both souls how to receive verbal attacks/criticisms, how to evaluate them in reference to their actions, change their actions if needed, and then put the experience behind them and prepare for the next attack/experience.

One soul proclaimed he felt ready to incarnate to the earth plane. The Masters and we angels agreed. So it was a happy day on earth when this soul appeared. He was the second child in this family and welcomed by all. His sister was five years older than he and was thrilled to be a part of 'mothering' him. She watched him grow and walk and talk. She wanted to be a part of everything he was learning in life. He was a very intelligent child and smiled and laughed when given the attention. All went well for him for many years. He developed a close relationship with his sister who felt it was her duty to always look after her little brother. Her little brother grew to be a very handsome and talented young man. She was very proud of him when he decided to enter medical school. He enjoyed life, studied hard and excelled in his studies, challenging many professors both in the classrooms and on the clinic floors. He loved life here with his fellow students and professors. Many times a group of them would get together for some drinks at a nearby pub. These were good times; they would recant their lectures or rounds for the day, laugh at each other and even support each other after a difficult test.

As the young man entered his second year of medical residency, he noticed he was becoming a little sluggish and clumsy. He shrugged it off to working many hours on the clinic floors. He tried to cover his clumsiness when others were around saying he tripped or he picked up a medical instrument the wrong way and it just fell out of his hand. He observed quietly what was happening to him. Some days were worse than others. It was getting more difficult to study the medical cases assigned to him. He was extremely tired. He begged off many offers to play basketball or go biking in the country saying he had a lot of work to catch up on. He finished his second year of residency with no one directly questioning his behavior. He had a few weeks off and returned home. His sister came to visit her brother at this time. After one evening of catching up with him, she knew something was wrong. She immediately thought he was using illegal drugs. She watched him carefully the few days they were together and decided to confront him when she saw how much he was sleeping and how he seemed to trip over everything and even nothing. Was he really 'stoned' she thought. While sitting on the front porch, she opened the conversation by asking what drugs he was using, why did he turn to drugs and for how long. He turned and just stared at her. WHAT, he said. She told him she immediately recognized he was different, that something was wrong with him. She said he looked and acted like he was high on drugs. He put his head down and said he didn't know it was that obvious. But, he continued, it's not drugs, like you think. Something is happening to me, to my body, he said. It started shortly after I started my second year residency. I worked to cover it up but I could see it was getting progressively worse. Right now I can hardly move. His sister looked him in the eyes and told him he was studying to be a doctor, a neurological doctor no less. She pointed out he was surrounded by medical experts. So why didn't you ask for help? If it is something that can be treated, she emphasized, you just lost about six months of treatment. You are so intelligent, why did you ignore this? He quietly said he was afraid. He did some investigation in his free time and he is suspecting progressive muscular degeneration. I don't want to give up the medical profession, he said with tears in his eyes. She said she understood his rationale but the time has come for him to face reality. She told him that he could possibly return to the medical profession once he understood and addressed his medical condition.

The young man's muscles continued to deteriorate. He was determined to finish his medical training. It was necessary for him to use a wheelchair as he finished the last part of his training. His co-workers were very fond of him and helped in any way they could …open a door, hand him a patient's chart, and many words of encouragement. However, the patient's were very skeptical when the doctor came to their hospital room sitting in a wheelchair. Many laughed and joked at him asking if he was tired from staying up all night partying. They thought he was just using the wheelchair for comfort. Some of their comments were cruel and many patients requested a doctor who could walk. The young doctor ignored many of these remarks but they were building inside of him. He hid these feelings because he was determined to become a doctor. He knew his mind was still strong and believed he could still help others despite his impending disability.

Upon completing many muscular and neurological evaluations, the medical school determined that with medication, the young doctor would be able to complete his residency at the medical center. He was elated. This last year was very difficult because he was expected to perform at the level of his co-workers. He was determined to succeed and complete all his medical training. He had no idea how hard this would be. The side effects of his medication contributed to his overall malaise. He questioned himself many times for this decision to continue but kept telling himself he could do it. As the months counted down to residency completion and the realization of making it to the end of his medical studies, the young doctor was slipping into depression. He needed a lot of physical help now, especially at home. His parents were there to help in every way possible...physical support, mental support, and even scholastic support. They researched medical journals for him when he needed information on different cases he was working on. He was extremely insightful on many medical conditions. His patients were always appreciative of his diagnosis and therapy even though they were very skeptical of a doctor who was in a wheelchair and had difficulty holding a pencil. He loved helping people and was able to draw enough energy from this satisfaction to survive each day at the hospital.

His guardian angels and I watched the young doctor very closely now. He was approaching a difficult time with this progressing handicap. We prepared him for this time period before he came to the earth plane, so we were very close to him now sending him messages and signs to call on us for help.

With the completion of his residency, he fell into a deeper depression. He was unable to secure a medical position to complete his career dreams. His muscles had deteriorated to where he needed physical therapy several times a week and professional help at home. He understood that if he could exercise his muscles daily, he would be able to stabilize his condition. However, the thought of giving up was growing in his mind. He had difficulty dealing with peoples' stares when he was out in public and the whispered comments about how he possibly came to this condition. He could sometimes hear these hushed comments. Was it drugs or violence, he overheard many times. He remembered his sister's reaction when she first saw that something was wrong with him. He was hurt. He wanted to scream and say I am a doctor not a criminal.

Those around him noticed him starting to withdraw. They said they understood but kept reminding him of his successes. We guided those trying to help him with messages to help pull him out of this withdrawal. This stage was the first big hurdle he needed to overcome. We could see that he was moving farther away from the help we were sending him. The angels who helped prepare him for this journey and I decided I would go down to try to help him pass this pivotal point.

I entered his life while he was in a physical therapy session. As I approached, I could hear him complaining about everything… his pain, his lack of success, his loss of independence, his inability to help others. With that statement, I stepped forward and asked him why he couldn't help others. He looked up surprised that someone was listening to him. By this time, all the workers had given up rationalizing his negative statements and trying to turn them to positive statements. I repeated my statement and he responded he couldn't do anything anymore without the use of his muscles. I looked him straight in the eyes and told him he still had his mind, his medical training and a great support group. Why are you feeling sorry for yourself, I asked. This shocked him because no one had ever accused him of feeling sorry for himself. He believed everyone felt sorry for himself but never thought it was vice-versa. We bantered back and forth with him always countering my positive statements of why he must make the effort to continue on with his life. Withdrawing from life, I told him strongly, should not be an option for anyone to escape the difficulties of life. With that being said, I told the young doctor if he ever needed help to call my name. It is Rashiel, I said. I then left the room.

The young man rallied some after my visit and began to rethink his life. Okay, he thought, I don't have my muscle strength anymore but my mind is still intact. I still have access to my mind. It is easier to withdraw from life with this type of condition, he thought, but what did that person in physical therapy mean that withdrawing should not be an option. This thought bothered the young man a lot and he was trying to rationalize that it didn't really apply to him because he experienced life to the fullest before this physical affliction. He was starting to feel sorry for himself again and started singing the same songs of woe as before. His sister visited him often and saw his mental deterioration. One day she was so exasperated she just shouted at him that she didn't feel sorry for him anymore because he was letting himself down. All the education you have, she said, is being wasted. We angels guided her eyes to a magazine on the table with a feature story of how an extremely crippled woman found a way to reach out and help those she believed were less fortunate than she. His sister suddenly pointed to the magazine and told her brother to read the article before he started on his sob stories again. She left him with the thought that withdrawing from life should not be an option for anyone no matter what a person is encountering. Remember, she said, there is always someone with greater difficulties than you.

We angels watched the young man very carefully now because the negative feelings were continuing. After a few days, he read the article and could not understand why or how this person wanted to survive let alone help others. He reread the article a few days later and as he did, we brought his attention to several statements about her disability that he could relate to. He then took a pen and highlighted the sections we were sending him signals on. He kept the article nearby for several days looking for answers not only for him but also for the female who wrote the article. He could not understand her thinking of how she accepted her disabilities. He finally shared his thoughts with his sister. She was elated to hear his interest in this article. While they discussed the similarities of the woman and the young man, we were feverishly sending messages to the young man to look at the bio of the woman particularly where she lived. He glanced down quickly at the end of their conversation and noticed the woman lived in the same town as he. He immediately commented to his sister he would like to meet her. His sister said she would make the arrangements.

Upon meeting the crippled woman, the young man was astonished. She was wheelchair bound and blind. She said she was blind from birth but a car accident left her paralyzed. She instinctively knew he was weak but that he could see. She told him she learned at an early age that blindness was a blessing to her and not a curse. How can that be, he asked. She told him it made her look at her strengths...she could hear extremely well, she could feel and sense almost any emotion in another person, and she is a college graduate. He then asked about her paralysis and how could something like that not affect her psyche. She told him that of course, it was difficult at first but she had a strong connection with her guardian angel from when she was a child and it was her guardian angel who led her to her present work of helping others less fortunate than she. She then asked the young man if he knew his guardian angel. He said no and never thought about anything spiritual helping him through this physical debilitation. She looked at him with the insight of really seeing him and told him he had better start talking to his guardian angel soon if he wanted to move on with his life. You are stuck, she said, I can feel it. Always remember, withdrawing from life should never be an option when facing the difficulties life can hand you. Please don't go there, she said. They talked a while longer and when he returned home, he truly felt rejuvenated.

Through his healing period of returning to help others, he did call on us angels many times. He remembered my name and called me to help him through some very dark thoughts. Rashiel, he cried out, I don't know if I can make it. I came immediately and he was startled when he opened his tearful eyes. Who are you, he said. I am an angel and you called me, I said. I am here to help you. It took a while before he was able to grasp the intensity of this visit but as he relaxed he cried profusely and told me all his fears. This was the first time he had ever confronted his true emotions. I assured him this was okay and was needed. Let the emotions pour out, I said, remove them from your body. When they are gone, I said, your healing will begin.

The young man made it through this pivotal point in his life and returned to what he loved, helping people. Once he progressed through all the stares and questions about his condition, he went on to become a great lecturer in the medical field. He held conferences not only for medical professionals but also for the general public. He especially loved these meetings because he knew he was truly helping many to manage or even overcome their illnesses and disabilities.

The young man remained on the earth plane for several years lecturing and helping others. His guardian angels were very happy to see him succeed. When he returned to us, there was great jubilation in heaven. His guardian angels, and the great Masters greeted him. When I walked over to him, he smiled and said 'thank you Rashiel, for coming to me. You helped me a lot'. We all walked him to God who smiled and welcomed him with opened arms. We knew this soul was strong enough to overcome the difficulties he chose but once the veil is dropped when a soul returns to earth, the outcome is always the result of free choice.

The second soul I prepared for a difficult task for his incarnation was not successful. This soul chose to be born with a defective spine. This very strong soul was counseled extensively. He was shown that a lot of physical difficulties would have to be overcome before he could begin to grow his soul in a productive life.

The boy's parents were told of his affliction when he was in the womb. They were disappointed but chose not to abort the baby. They believed this soul had a right to a chance on earth and they wanted to give the child an environment of total love. The hospital, doctors, and parents were prepared when the soul arrived on the earth plane. The baby was immediately put on life sustaining equipment. The doctors knew the first forty-eight hours were crucial for the child to survive. If he made it, they believed he could live for many years given the proper physical rehabilitation. The parents and family members knew these risks and all sent many prayers to God to help this child through this difficult and dangerous period.

The soul contacted us many times during this period, going in and out of his body. He had many doubts now of his decision to incarnate under these circumstances. We supported him as he told us his fears. We reviewed all the counseling sessions we had with him pointing out how he kept assuring us he could do it. He responded he could now see how truly difficult this task was. He said he could see it more clearly since he incarnated. As the time on earth moved on during those early days, his doubts became stronger. We kept telling him he was an experienced, strong soul but his cries became louder. Finally, he made the decision. He stated he wanted to come back to us. At that point, his guardian angels and I had to stand aside. He exercised free will, which we honor. It was his choice to leave his earthly body and return to us. Once the decision was made, we prepared to receive this soul back in heaven.

All of us angels, who worked with him, greeted him warmly when he returned. He apologized profusely because he felt he let us down. He believed he had failed. We assured him he did not fail. We were proud of him for trying and having the courage to stop the process when he realized it was too difficult a task for him at this time in his soul development. What will God think of me because I failed, he asked. God doesn't evaluate you as succeeding or failing, we said. God loves you and admires you for the work you are doing to develop your soul to move closer to Him. God knows you will try again. Just then the soul looked up and saw God opening his arms out to him. God then smiled, whispered 'welcome home' and lovingly held the soul in His arms.

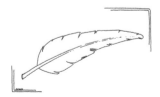

DONYERNE

I AM DONYERNE. I AM an archangel but not known on the earth plane. I am with the angels who monitor violence on earth. Although there has always been violence on this planet, it is through this violence and the struggles it causes to humankind that spirits work to develop their souls. They learn to overcome the cause or causes of violence while on the earth plane or by helping others overcome violent behaviors. Once a soul has experienced violence, and transitions through it, often it will choose to return to earth to help others achieve peace when involved in violent situations. Souls are taught that violence erupts from many causes. Many of these causes include hatred, selfishness, jealousy, greed, and pride. Each soul who chooses to experience a violent period in their life on earth is coached extensively on how to recognize their behavior, whether they were the cause of a violent reaction with their words or actions or whether they just reacted to another's confrontational behavior. This teaching process is very important for the soul to remember in order to survive.

Violence extends from global war to neighborhood skirmishes to domestic events. We prepare the souls thoroughly for what they may encounter on the earth plane in forms of violence.

I worked extensively with a female soul because she had experienced violence several times in her journeys to earth. With this incarnation, she was determined to remove the hatred in her heart that she carried with her on several incarnations. She was the first-born child to a very young couple. They were too immature at this time to accept the responsibility of raising another human being. Both their parents were very supportive of the marriage and pregnancy because they each wanted a grandchild. It was a great day for the entire family when the baby arrived on the earth plane. Her parents were in absolute awe of this little human being. The little girl was cared for and smothered with love from her paternal and maternal grandparents. Her parents were able to return to their everyday world of work and play because of the support of the grandparents. Thus, the parents readily returned to their independent living they enjoyed before the baby was born. They started to resent the nighttime cries when the baby was sick or woke up frightened from a dream. On the weekends, the parents argued about who would tend to their daughter so the other could be free to explore their own life interests. They called on the grandparents many, many times to watch the baby so they could have time together without tending to the needs of the child. The young parents were showing many signs of resenting the presence of their little girl. They were not ready to have a child in their lives now but the grandparents were hoping the child would help them mature more quickly and easily.

The grandparents saw how the parents grew apart from their little girl year by year. The distance was obvious not only to the grandparents but also to other members of the family and friends. The family discussed the impact this environment was having on the child many times but did not know how to intercede. The grandparents talked to their children in hopes of getting them professional help. The little girl's personality was changing. She didn't smile and laugh as she used to. She cried a lot saying that no one loved her. She felt ugly and rejected. The grandparents decided to spend as much time with the little girl as possible. They all worked to smother her with love but each set of grandparents wanted to outdo the other so they equated love with toys and clothes. By the time the little girl was in grade school, she knew for sure her parents didn't like her and she could get anything she wanted from her grandparents. Her behavior changed dramatically as she progressed through school. She became outspoken and demanding to her classmates. She was looking for love and friendship and believed she could demand it from her peers just as she demanded toys from her grandparents.

The young girl's parents looked at their daughter's behavior and now decided to step back into her life. They tried to be a part of her life as a teenager but the young girl would have no part of them. She wanted to hurt them as much as she believed they hurt her. She had no love for them. She thought about it one day and decided that she truly did hate them for their lack of love and attention during her early years. She felt the hatred rising in her heart not only against her parents but also against the classmates who rejected her.

All the angels who worked with this soul knew she was coming to a very critical time in her life where she wanted to overcome the hatred she had experienced so many times in previous lives. She was not working with her guardian angels anymore. Both sets of grandparents talked extensively about angels when she was a little girl. They taught her to talk to them daily and call on them whenever she was sad or needed help. Her guardian angels were now sending her many messages and signs hoping she would turn to them for help and guidance. But the young girl chose to keep her heart closed to the angels.

The young girl was determined to graduate from high school with high honors despite her offensive personality. She now believed everyone in school was against her but she wanted to show that she was better than they. To achieve this, she worked to excel in all her classes and became Valedictorian.

She was presented many awards and a full scholarship to a prominent college. Her parents were very proud of her success and believed they had raised a beautiful, loving child. But the young woman was still struggling with the hate she had in her heart for her parents. Their congratulatory hugs and tears were met with stiffness and a cold stare as she whispered 'why don't you love me'? She turned and walked away.

At college, the young girl again excelled in her coursework. She was a loner and still looked cautiously at anyone trying to be friendly to her. She liked being alone and by now, her heart was turning to stone. She found herself believing she was not capable of love. She was convinced it was not needed in life because she had successfully survived thus far without it. She didn't cry anymore, not even at sad movies. She started going to more violent movies. The more sinister, backstabbing, and violent, the more she enjoyed it. While at college, the young girl did not stay in contact with her family, not even her grandparents.

The young girl's guardian angels were working feverishly to come into her life as they watched her move farther away from God and closer to hatred and violence. They directed a young man to come into her life. He had a very strong personality with a heart open to God and the angels. He intrigued her primarily because she could not dominate nor intimidate him. He could see her struggling with love and hate. He was a little frightened with how much hate was in her heart and proceeded cautiously and slowly to get to know her. He wanted to know her deep secrets and hurt. She pushed him away many times but he always returned to her, sometimes months later.

She continued going to bizarre and violent movies identifying with the hatred she saw on the screen. The violence seemed to relieve some of the feelings in her heart but only temporarily. She watched the moviegoers many times as they exited the theater looking at their faces and wondering why they went to violent movies. Were there a lot of people like her in this world? She concluded there must be because these types of movies were gaining in popularity. The young man she had befriended went with her to one of these bizarre movies. He could see how she thrived on the violent scenes. They discussed several of the scenes many times and he worked to differentiate love and hate as seen in the movie. It was the first time he was able to open this type of conversation with her. She stiffened and lashed out at him with a powerful retort that there is no loves on this planet, only hate. He took a deep breath, whispered for help from the angels, and proceeded to show her where love existed even in the most violent scene. This was difficult for her so she left immediately and asked him to stay out of her life.

The unrest in the world intrigued her. She loved reading about violence that extended from war zones to neighborhood fights and murders. She felt she could identify with the hate involved between nations and neighbors. They all had a right to fight and kill, she thought. Why should they try to care and love one another and mend their grievances? She wrote many articles in the school newspaper supporting this right to fight and kill. Some articles were very radical and most seemed to have justification for the existence of hatred in the world. As her articles grew more radical, she attracted a following that supported her ideals. They would meet several times a week to discuss local and world violent events. Love was not in their hearts, only hate. These educated people wanted to destroy.

We angels decided the young girl needed help, for she had drifted very far off course from her plan to rid her heart of hate. I walked into one of the off-campus gatherings with this group and sat nearby listening. They worked very hard to justify recent violent actions. No one noticed me until I stood up and asked if anyone ever thought about the harm these hateful acts were doing to the innocent people? They all looked surprised at this statement. Several voices hollered in unison 'who cares'. I asked them to close their eyes and imagine they were the victims receiving mental and physical attacks. How do you feel being on the receiving end? The young woman stood up and looked me in the eyes and said that she was already there. She said her whole life was filled with hurt. She felt she had every right to strike back at everyone and anyone whom she felt didn't like her. I asked her, 'how are they able to like you if you refuse to open your heart to them'. My heart is closed, she exclaimed. My friends accept me the way I am. And how many true friends do you have, I asked. She lowered her eyes and did not answer. Who are you, she exclaimed. You obviously are not one of us. No, I said, I am not with your group. I am with your angels who are trying very hard to open your cold heart and help you receive God into your life. My name is Donyerne. When I announced my name, she became enraged and walked out the door.

The young girl continued in life as a journalist. She secured a job with a well-respected news company and worked her way through the ranks by stepping on and degrading many other talented journalists. She was disliked by her peers but respected for her journalistic talent. She grew famous for her reporting because many liked the way she could dissect violence. She always emphasized that hatred was a part of violence and those that hated had rights. Many other journalists started to strike at her for her belief that if one hated and caused injury to another, that person had a right or just cause to be violent. A rebellion seemed to be rising in the journalistic world. One journalist, who was very strong and well respected, decided to campaign against the writings of the young girl. He remembered her from college, her cold heart, and how he felt drawn to her for some reason. He felt this feeling again but this time he knew it was necessary to take a stand against her. Several journalists had tried this already but she destroyed their careers.

As he countered her articles one by one when they were published, the young woman took notice and the hatred in her heart began to rise. She sought him out one evening after a press conference but didn't recognize him. She said that she would destroy him. He asked why didn't she remember him. Was her heart that cold that she wouldn't even remember some of the good times they had together in college, he asked. She stared at him and then a faint smile crossed her face. I remember, she said, you were determined to teach me about love. You are strong, but I will still destroy you, she whispered. The young man shook his head no and whispered he had Special Forces on his side...God and His angels. She stormed out.

The young man talked daily to the angels for support because he knew he was being guided to help this young woman. He kept telling himself not to give up even when her attacks on him escalated. He kept asking for direction from the angels. At this point, we stepped in. We sent him many signs and messages, which he received willingly. His confidence increased. We inspired him to write an article about her that outlined her hate from early childhood to the development of a person who was able to destroy many lives and families.

He followed our direction and wrote an open article to her addressing her destructive personality. The only way to stop this hatred in your heart, he wrote, is to look deep inside your heart, look at your hatred, look at your hurt and cry. Yes, cry to release all your hurt. Then, look in the mirror, look into your eyes – look into your soul. Look deep and feel the hurt that has engulfed you and feel the hurt you caused others. You wanted to hurt them, as you were hurt. After you acknowledge and release this hurt, you must forgive those who you perceived did injury to you. Study how your hurt turned to hatred. Then study how your hatred turned to destruction – destruction of all who crossed your path and failed to admire and support you. Now study how much you are destroying yourself. You have no love in your heart. No love for yourself, no love for your peers, and especially no love for your family. Look at your cold heart. Do you like the way you are? Do you like how you destroy people's lives - emotionally and financially? Do you like how much sadness you have brought to your parents and grandparents? Life is all about being happy; feeling love, enjoying all that God has given you. But you have made life very ugly for yourself as well as for all those around you including your family. I tried to show you love a long time ago but you cast me out of your life. Well, I feel I have been guided to help you again to open your heart to love, to God. The young man signed the article and whispered a prayer to us that his words not fall on deaf ears.

We angels watched very carefully now because this was a critical point in the young girl's life if she were to begin to remove hate from her heart and return to God. Her guardian angels were with her constantly sending her many messages and signs to help bring about the change. The messages were always returned to the angels because she refused to open her heart and hear their voices.

The young girl was absolutely furious when she read the article. Her anger was so strong she wanted to physically harm the young man. She started to remember the violent movies she would watch as a college student and the satisfaction she experienced when hatred and violence prevailed. These thoughts were getting stronger and more frequent the more she thought about the article written to her. She felt she had to respond to the young man but not with written words. She arranged to meet him in a park one afternoon. He was sitting very confidently on a park bench and even smiled as she approached. She was seething when she saw his smile but knew she had to keep her feelings controlled. They exchanged pleasantries and then the bantering began. Guardian angels as well as archangels surrounded them. He could see her anger escalating as she described his audacity at writing such an article. He let her talk and scream at him for as long as she needed. He knew she was venting long, repressed anger and hurt. Finally, she stopped and just stared at him and asked why he wasn't arguing back. He asked her to remember the article where she should scream and cry to remove all the hate in her heart. Now she felt like he set a trap for her and her emotions exploded again. Her fists were clenched now and he knew she was closing herself off to him. He quietly asked her to just acknowledge her guardian angels, just this once, he said. They will help you through this. She responded loudly that she did not want any help from him or his angels regarding her life. She was doing just fine, she said. They will send you signs, look for them, he said. She looked at him like he was really crazy. She wanted to end this conversation and stood to leave. At that moment, a feather drifted down and landed by her foot. The young man pointed to the feather and told her she had just received a sign from her guardian angels. He picked it up and handed it to her. She looked at it skeptically and opened her hand to receive it. As she turned and rushed off, he hollered for her to look for more angel signs.

Back at the office, she looked at the feather and then threw it on her desk. He was trying to trick me, she thought. Just then, a co-worker walked in, pointed to the feather and said he loved receiving signs from the angels. She was ready to explode, feeling a conspiracy around her involving angels and love. She remembered the afternoon in the park - there was neither love in her heart nor any angels floating around. She acknowledged to herself that she truly wanted to destroy him. Her hatred was growing again. She looked at the feather on her desk but instead of throwing it in the trash can she put it in a drawer. As she closed the drawer, she remembered her grandmother telling her about the angels and if they send you a feather, keep it close because they are talking to you. She quickly dismissed the thought.

At the grocery store, shortly after her meeting in the park, she overheard two customers talking about angels. She listened to their conversation for several minutes and was intrigued they both knew the names of their guardian angels and how much the angels influenced their lives. This is nonsense, she thought. However, she did feel an incredible feeling of peace come over her by just standing next to them. She tried to dismiss this feeling. She turned away but looked back immediately for one last glance but they were gone. Where did they go, she thought, how did they leave so quickly.

In the days following her meeting with the young man in the park, she tried feverishly to destroy his journalistic career. She was successful in destroying others; she would add him to her list. But each time she started an article against him, she was interrupted. First it was the phone, then a meeting, travel, appearances, and dinners. The list never seemed to end. However, she made a mental note of this project and swore to herself she would complete it. It wasn't over for her, she thought. At the local journalistic award ceremony, she found herself on the stage standing next to the young man. He smiled graciously and said hello. She smiled a little but whispered carefully she was going to destroy him. He laughed and told her she couldn't because he had an army of angels on his side. She just glared at him. During dinner, he asked if she received any more angel signs. She said no and that she wasn't looking. Right then, a journalist approached her and asked if she would do a story about a little girl who was rejected by her parents, lived with her grandparents and called on her angels every day asking why her parents didn't love her. The young man just stared at the journalist and then at the young woman. At that moment, he knew this journalist was an angel. The young woman asked for details about the story but said she didn't think it was exciting enough for her to write about. The young man exclaimed this would be a great humanitarian story. He said that people who read the story would open their hearts to give love to the little girl. But, I understand, he said, your image, as a snake journalist, would change significantly. Her feelings of hate for him were rising once again. She felt trapped. To save face with this journalist, she consented to interview the little girl and possibly write the story.

The young woman met with the little girl several times at her grandparents home. The little girl was five years old and very articulate with her feelings of love for her parents who just abandoned her. She said it looked like she was not wanted by them and they didn't love her but she knew differently. When asked how she knew this, she responded her guardian angel told her. The young woman stopped, realizing angels were coming back into her life. They just won't stop, she thought. She decided at that point never to let angels into her life. But then, she heard the little girl say that she actually sees her guardian angel and her angel's name is Belinda. The young woman continued the interviews and slowly wrote the story struggling with the presence of love and angels as the main theme. She concluded the story by admitting that it was truly love that will guide the little girl through life. As she was writing, the young woman had glimpses of her life, remembering abandonment at a very young age. She tried to dismiss these thoughts but they kept returning with the picture of how the little girl was dealing with the same feelings. I have learned to hate because of my childhood, she finally acknowledged to herself.

The young woman's guardian angels were ecstatic. They believed she was going to make her way back to love. We need to help her open her heart to God, they said.

The young woman continued on with her career and received many more awards for her journalistic skills and a special humanitarian award. She was not yet opening to the angels but was feeling more comfortable talking about them as they occurred in her story. The young man showed up in her life again when the story was published. He congratulated her and asked if she knew her guardian angel's name. She started to get angry with him but the anger subsided. She suddenly saw him differently. She felt a calm come over her as she stood near him. This time she looked into his eyes and saw total love. She smiled and asked, with a little sarcasm, if he was her guardian angel. He smiled and shook his head yes. She just stared at him. Okay, so if you are an angel, what is your name, she asked. I never heard of angels having names until I wrote that story of the little girl and she told me her guardian angel's name. My name is Broznier, he responded. Do you have a last name to identify what group of angels you come from, she asked. He laughed and said no. If you need me, he said, just call my name and I will hear you.

The young woman continued on with her career but still had a strong tendency to hurt those who crossed her path and didn't agree with her writings. We watched carefully as the hate started to rise in her heart again. Our messages were again falling on deaf ears and a closed heart. One day, she got word the little girl in her humanitarian story was in the hospital. She felt a little sad but shrugged it off. She probably got the flu or something, she thought. We worked desperately to direct her attention to the hospital where the little girl was a patient. There was political controversy occurring at the hospital so the young journalist decided to research the story. While at the hospital, she wandered around the different floors trying to overhear any conversation from the staff regarding the hospital. On the fifth floor she saw the little girl in her story lying in a bed in the hallway. The little girl had bandages over most of her body. The young journalist just stopped and stared in disbelief. What could have happened to this beautiful child who adored her grandparents and forgave her parents for not wanting her. The little girl turned her head and smiled when she saw the young journalist. She could not talk because her face was too swollen. A nurse came up just then and asked the young journalist if she was a relative of the little girl. The journalist shook her head no and with tears asked the nurse if she knew what happened. The nurse said a neighborhood gang beat the little girl. They wanted to bring grief to her parents who they felt cheated them of drug money. The nurse continued to say that no one has been in to visit the little girl since she arrived. Where are her grandparents, the journalist asked. They were frightened when this happened and feared they would also be injured if they showed any interest in the little girl. So everyone is just abandoning this beautiful child, she asked? Yes, the nurse responded. Choking back the tears, the young journalist approached the little girl. She looked up with total love in her eyes. The young journalist asked if the little girl was talking to her angel, Belinda. The little girl shook her head yes. Are you angry, she asked. The little girl shook her head no. And tell me you don't hate your parents and the boys who did this to you? Again the little girl shook her head no. I don't understand, she said to the little girl. The young journalist then kissed the little girl on her forehead, said she loved her, and she would be back to visit. The little girl's eyes swelled with tears and a faint smile was on her face.

The young journalist left the hospital and walked for several blocks trying to understand all she had just witnessed. Why did the little girl love so much? With all the injury she had experienced, mentally and physically, where was her hate? She believed the little girl had to develop hate to strengthen and prepare her to face the world. She sat down on a bench in the park nearby to try to make sense of this love in the little girl's heart. She reviewed the parallels of their lives except she developed hate and the little girl developed love. She closed her eyes and without realizing it whispered Broznier's name. Within the minute, Broznier came and quietly sat next to the young journalist. He waited until she opened her eyes and said he was there to help her. Yes, she said, I want the love I see in that little girl's heart. I just don't understand. She has experienced so much more rejection than I. She must hurt tremendously inside but her love is admirable. I want to do the same but I don't think I can, she said to Broznier. Nothing is impossible, especially with God and His angels, he responded. What do I do, where do I start, she asked. I have hated for so long and destroyed so many, I am surprised the angels are still hanging around me. He laughed and said that no one is never too far away from God that he can't return. That is why I am here. You called me. I can see you are starting to open your heart to God and hear our voices. That is the beginning but it is the hardest part of returning to us. It is easier to return to your feelings of hate. You were comfortable there but you were not happy. You knew you were not happy so you surrounded yourself with destructive acts. You equated those acts with satisfaction and happiness. We angels were always with you but you refused to hear or see us. We were successful in bringing the little girl to you. You almost said no. We also directed you to the hospital because the little girl was there. We were hoping that if you could see her life struggles and her love, you would see the difference between her and you. She did open your heart and now you can truly start to experience God's love here on earth. But, he said, again this is your choice. The young journalist listened quietly, her heart breaking now as she looked at her destructive life. She asked Broznier again, 'do I have a chance with God'? He smiled and said yes. They sat on the bench discussing her past life and how she can remove the hate in her heart.

The young journalist returned to the hospital a few days later to visit the little girl. When she walked into the room, the little girl lit up with joy as she recognized the journalist. She very proudly introduced her parents and grandparents. The young journalist quickly evaluated the scenario, wondering how this could be but decided to go with the love that was in the room. The parents and grandparents thanked the journalist for the beautiful story she wrote about the little girl. They assured the journalist that it was through this story and the love in the heart of their little girl that changed their lives. The young journalist was deeply moved. She left the room knowing her return to love had begun.

The young journalist continued through life struggling to change. This was a slow process because she had hurt and destroyed so many people in her life. She had an almost indelible reputation of destruction. She realized this and with determination slowly changed. She opened her heart to God and us angels and learned to hear our voices in her heart. She changed her journalistic style from acrid to humanitarian. She campaigned now for the underprivileged and neglected children. She was criticized by many saying she had an agenda to further her career and would somehow hurt those she was campaigning for. She continued feverishly to change her reputation. She made restitution when she could to those she injured. The young woman then knew she was ready to go home. She walked slowly into her parents' home and said 'hello'. They screamed and ran to her with open arms and it was at that moment she truly saw the love in their hearts for her.

When she returned here to heaven, there was great celebration. Broznier and I entered as she smiled shyly and said 'thank you' both for being so persistent. She then thanked all the angels surrounding her for never giving up on her. She was extremely grateful for all the guidance we provided because she knew she was close to not succeeding in removing her hatred. But she was successful and there was much celebration here in heaven. We all surrounded this spirit as she walked toward God who wrapped His arms around her and whispered 'welcome back and congratulations'. She was now totally surrounded with love.

SCHIENTELLE

I AM CALLED SCHIENTELLE AND I am with the corps of angels who monitor the health of the earth plane. This may sound frivolous and unnecessary to you but in order for you to continue to survive on earth, your environment must be healthy. The planet earth is constantly evolving. Your history books will attest to how dramatically the earth has changed based on archeological findings. Life it once supported no longer exists due to successive environmental changes. The planet earth has cleansed itself many times because it was severely polluted and weak. Presently, you witness many environmental purges such as volcano eruptions, earthquakes, hurricanes, cyclones, tornadoes, and extreme rain or snow. The earth is a living entity and must be respected if life is to continue on this planet.

There are many angels assigned to protect and guard the earth. You may identify us as 'earth's guardian angels'. So you say, 'exactly WHAT is the role of an earth angel'? We watch the health of the earth's environment by monitoring vegetated health, atmospheric health, sea health, animal health, and human health. We carefully monitor all factors affecting these areas. The planet itself is able to send us many distress signals. When we receive these types of signals, we are on high alert because we know the earth is preparing to do a purge and rid itself of harmful poisons. For example, if the poisons are in the atmosphere, the earth may cleanse itself with a powerful rainstorm. The poisons or toxins will be cleansed from the air but you will say they are being washed into the soil, rivers, and oceans. That is true but the earth primarily needs to cleanse its air first. A rainstorm dilutes these toxins that are being washed into the earth. The atmosphere is cleansed and more oxygen becomes available for all life forms. However, the diluted toxins that enter the earth will gradually accumulate and the earth will eventually purge itself of these toxins and all other toxins that have moved into its soils and waterways. So, as you can see, this is a never-ending cycle.

As we monitor the earth in all areas, we can see where eruptions will occur and how devastating they will be. We send many messages to the human population warning them to get out of harm's way. We cannot stop the earth from its purging process but we can help all those who will be affected by it. Many souls return to the earth plane with the written plan to help the human race. These spirits return to be caretakers, educators, and still others to advance environmental science.

I recently had a spirit come to our angel corps to observe how we monitor the earth… the signs and messages we send to earth before an impending earth incident. He came to us to study how we work together as a group to contact humans to alert them to impending earthly disasters. He said he wanted to remember all we were teaching him because he intended to incarnate to work to save Mother Earth from human destruction. We looked at this spirit and reminded him this was a powerful plan for one soul. He responded that he realized the enormity of this incarnation and added he was working with several great Masters to prepare him for the obstacles that would confront him. This was a very advanced spirit who decided to return to earth specifically to educate and advance earth's scientific world regarding cleaning up the earth's environment.

As this soul progressed through childhood on the earth plane, he showed great interest in animals and insects especially those who appeared sickly. He tried very hard to understand at his young age why some animals, insects and even fish would suddenly die in large numbers. He felt sad when he heard this information on the news. He independently studied insect lifecycles. He looked very closely at nesting birds, turtles, and an array of other small animals. His parents encouraged their son in all that he pursued in nature. In school, his nature projects won many awards. He was very happy to observe and assist with any animal, bird or insect that crossed his path. As he progressed through school, he was seen many times by himself reading or walking or even just sitting by the river near his house. Not many of his classmates held the same interests as he. By the time he reached high school, he was labeled as a 'loner'. His parents became a little concerned with his lack of friends but thought he would grow away from his love for nature and become more aware of school activities. Because they believed he was capable of learning how to catch or throw a ball or to swim, they encouraged him to participate in sports. They wanted him to get involved to expand his social circle. He tried a couple of sports but just fell flat. He was totally uncoordinated. His classmates laughed and called him a 'nerd'. He was angry at their jeering and name-calling and withdrew from his classmates even more. He asked his parents to stop pushing him into areas he was not comfortable. They honored his request for they could see his anger had turned to hurt; this pained them very much. They loved their son and just wanted to see him succeed in life surrounded by good friends. They tried to protect him from insults as much as they could. But this hovering caused him to distance himself from his parents. He was very lonely and unhappy at home and school. However, turning to nature always brought him peace and happiness. He did not know why but he felt a drawing to nature as though it was a magnet he could not resist.

As he walked along a nature path near his home, he felt himself getting stronger inside. He looked at himself and at his classmates and knew he was different but not in the way they perceived him. He knew they saw him as stupid, awkward, and socially inept. The longer he walked, the stronger he got. He started to see inside himself. He saw a person who was caring, aware and in love with all of God's beings. Why can't they see what I see, he wondered. There is so much beauty on earth. I accept that I am different, he said to himself, and I like myself this way. At that moment he decided to study nature in college and become an expert in preserving God's beautiful earth.

He graduated from high school with high honors in science. He ended his valedictorian speech telling all present in the auditorium they had the responsibility to preserve the beautiful earth that has served them for many years. This became his mantra for all his projects in college.

Life was not as lonely for him in college as it was in high school. He made friends with many who shared his intelligence and beliefs. They would sit for many hours discussing and debating the cause and effect of recent catastrophes. It was through these debates that he realized the effect pollution might have on the earth. He gravitated toward environmental studies and worked endlessly on many theories and projects. He would stay at school working on his projects sometimes using his sleeping bag to rest a few hours not wanting to return to his room for food and sleep. He believed he was making progress in proving his theories but he was also losing weight and sleep in this process. His instructors noticed this change. They encouraged him to slow down since he had one more year of undergraduate work and he could carry all this work into a graduate program. He knew they were right but he was becoming totally obsessed with his thoughts. He had six separate projects in process at this time and more ideas were coming to him. His advisor suggested that he leave the college and take a vacation during spring break. The young man looked panicky with this suggestion. He believed if he left his work for ten days the data wouldn't be current and therefore he could not use it. The professor said this was not the case because his research did not require that kind of data recording.

The young man reluctantly returned to his hometown. He was received with open arms from his family but they were immediately concerned. He was very thin and frail. What was going on, they thought. His parents immediately took him under their wing and worked feverishly to nourish and love him. He struggled at first with this attention, but then settled in, as it seemed like a warm security blanket. He talked endlessly about his research and how he had an undying drive to prove to the science world the effect the ecosystem has on the health of the earth system. His parents were impressed with his enthusiasm but had many doubts he would be able to convince the world to change the pollution problem. Their son was so intense on this area of global pollution he could not let it go to relax while away from school. This worried his parents. If their son was this intense in undergraduate school, how would he be in graduate school and even postgraduate school? They worried but knew they could not talk to their son about relaxing and forgetting his studies even for ten days.

The young man graduated with distinction from college and received several grants from graduate schools for work in environmental studies. He was elated. He felt he was on the path to success. People were starting to listen to his theories. He progressed through graduate school with great success and received many acknowledgements from the academic world. However, he knew he needed to address the world outside academia so he accepted employment with a very reputable environmental company. After a few months, the young man realized much of the environmental data was 'fitted' into graphs and charts to satisfy what the majority of the world was looking for. This was not acceptable, he thought. World pollution is killing the earth and he needed to tell the world. Where to start? What country in the world was the worst? Which was the best? What are the signs the earth gives us that tell us where pollution is highest? It is all here in my work, he said to himself. I just need to show the analysis with charts and graphs. He started work on this project without telling anyone in the company. I must do this, he thought, because I know I can help the world.

He watched carefully the violent earth occurrences around the world – volcanoes erupting, massive flooding, hurricanes, cyclones, tornadoes, earthquakes, tsunamis and many more. He put these eruptions on a graph along with the level of air, sea, and land pollution and he could clearly see a pattern. He was elated. All his previous thinking and predictions were coming to fruition. It is true; he rationalized. Humans ARE causing these violent earthly incidents. If we cleanse the earth, we can live in a perfect and beautiful environment. The young man now became obsessed with his theories and worked endlessly to prove his research work. Those who worked closely with him believed in him and encouraged him to advance his theories to the higher levels. He worked endlessly but the higher he took his research, the harder it was to convince the corporate world. The upper echelon of the world-renowned company did not want to ruffle feathers especially on a world level. They told him to keep his ideas to himself. The young scientist was flabbergasted. He could not believe his research was going to be totally ignored and that the world would continue without recognizing the effect of pollution on the environment. 'We are going to annihilate ourselves if we don't change' he related to fellow researchers. The young man became totally frustrated at how the world could be so unaware of the damage it was doing to its environment.

The young scientist left the world-renowned company to try to announce to the world himself the dangers of pollution.

Many earth-loving groups engaged the young man to speak at special gatherings. This was encouraging but the young man realized this was still not enough. It was just bringing awareness. But he continued with these engagements. Maybe there would be just one person in the audience who would realize the magnitude of his subject and be in a position to bring it to global recognition. He received notoriety following several of his speaking engagements. However, with this small fame came a following of environmental extremists. He liked to engage with them and even spar with them at public gatherings but he did not see their extremist views nor their shallowness and selfishness. They viewed the young man as a spokesperson for their causes. The causes they focused on were directed to destroy community and government programs. The young scientist was easily pulled into the group and was able to make presentations to small community gatherings as well as to some very significant organizations. He was very happy belonging to this group and being its spokesperson. He had no idea how destructive they were. He continued in this role for many months traveling the world with his messages.

The young man sat in his room one morning staring at the headlines in a national newspaper. The group he represented was exposed as a fraud working to destroy the world's societies. His name was emblazoned as the leader. The article continued to unravel all his environmental theories linking them to instilling fear into the human race. He was labeled as the 'doomsday' scientist. His whole world came crashing down around him as he sat alone in his room in a far-away city. Tears rolled down his cheeks. I am not a bad person, he kept telling himself. I only want to help save the earth for future generations, he thought. I am trying to open everyone's eyes to the potentially destructive effects of pollution, and how to clean it up. He just wanted to scream the truth to the world.

His career was over and he knew it. There was a knock at the door and in burst the news media. He did not know how to handle the chaos. He just wanted to run. When he finally escaped, he started to walk as he did as a child to be close to nature. We angels watched him closely now for he was dangerously close to self-destruction. We walked with him, sending him messages and signs along the trail. Please hear us, we whispered. Open your heart to us; we will guide you through this difficult time. As a child, the young man learned to recognize our signs along his nature walk. He always loved to find a feather along the path. He would pick it up, look at it closely, smile and look up and whisper 'thank you'. Now, in his distraught state, he walked by several feathers we sent to him. We sent a gentle breeze through the trees hoping he would look to the sky and see some forms of angels in the clouds. He just continued on with his head bowed low and tears streaming from his eyes. We heard him saying to himself how sorry he was that he caused so much depression in the world. He truly believed he convinced the world population the earth was going to self-destruct. Who were these people he joined, he wondered. What was their purpose in using him to gain popularity and trust? Are they truly destructive? How did they destroy? I just don't understand, he kept repeating. Why did I not see their hardened hearts? He walked and walked for several hours moving deeper and deeper into depression. We continued sending him messages and signs, but he would not open his heart to us.

As he walked deeper into the wooded area, a man on a bicycle approached him. With his eyes focused on the ground, the young man almost walked into the biker. The startled scientist suddenly looked up to see who was hollering and why. The biker quieted as soon as he saw the sad man with tears still streaming down his face. The biker looked the young man directly into his eyes and asked if he could give him a shoulder to lean on. The young man broke down completely saying he had nothing to live for now, his career was over. The biker immediately got off his bike and put both arms around the young man. The biker didn't say anything but slowly walked his saddened companion to a nearby bench. He let the young man cry his heart out whispering softly how the angels loved him. The young man became very quiet and looked directly into the biker's eyes and said without hesitation, 'you are an angel, aren't you'? The biker answered he was just responding to someone who is in need of help. No, the young man said, you talked about angels. I heard you tell me how much they love me. And I did, responded the biker, but that doesn't necessarily mean that I am an angel. I guess it doesn't, he responded. I think I was just hoping against hope. You see, I grew up talking to the angels every day especially when I was alone in the fields or by the river. I always felt them around me. But, I guess, I grew away from them. I got very busy at school and now this. But if they are always with me, how did this happen to me? I am ruined; my career is over. I thought they would always protect me. They do, the biker responded, but you also have free will and can always choose the opposite of your angels' messages. If you were close to the angels as a child and teen, then surely you recognized the messages they sent to you. I'm sure you could also hear their messages in your heart. The young man sat quietly and slowly shook his head yes. What happened, he asked the biker. I was doing so well. I had a very promising career. Large corporations were gradually accepting my theories about the detrimental effects of pollution on the environment. How did I get mixed up with such a destructive group and believe I was going to save the world single-handedly? You did have signs, the biker said. They were all around you but you chose to ignore them. Think carefully now about the first meeting with the leader of this group. Think of the signs and messages you received and ignored. I remember, he said, they canceled the first two meetings. No reason was given. I was disappointed but pushed for another meeting. I remember feeling I should leave that third meeting, but I didn't. I really wanted notoriety at that time. So you see, the biker said, the angels were there but YOU chose to ignore them. If you think carefully about the time you spent with this group, travelling the world, living the good life, you will see many, many more instances where the angels were communicating with you. I want you to visualize those instances and see how you exercised free will and the directions those choices took you.

The two men sat on the bench analyzing the young man's life for several hours. This was a very critical time for the young man. We angels were watching to see if he would make the decision to stay on the earth plane to complete his life's plan. The young man asked the biker his name. He said to just call him Schientelle. How can I contact you, he asked. Don't worry, Schientelle said, when you need me, I will be there for you. With that, he quickly disappeared on his bike. The young man sat on the bench a little longer analyzing his conversation with Schientelle. As he walked back to his apartment, he felt stronger and even happier. He sensed a quiet peace in his heart.

His name was cleared as being a leading voice for the notorious group. He quietly returned to his alma mater and secured a position in the environmental department. He worked quietly and reacquainted himself with his angels. He talked to them daily just as he did as a child. They were simple conversations but whenever he got stuck on a project he asked the angels for help. They were always there for him. He was happy now and he truly believed his happiness came from working with the angels.

Schientelle was the first angel to greet the scientist when he returned to heaven. Schientelle smiled, hugged the scientist and welcomed him back home. The scientist recognized Schientelle and said 'thank you' for helping me complete my life plan but I don't believe I was successful. Schientelle pointed to a large room on the earth plane and said 'listen, they are discussing your theories. They are putting them into action. The earth is getting cleaned up; it will survive. We are very proud of you.' He heard great music at that time and saw a bright light moving toward him. Schientelle stepped aside as God extended His arms to congratulate the young man and welcome him back home.

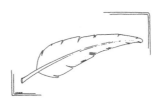

DONRIALE

I WOULD LIKE TO INTRODUCE myself. I am Archangel Donriale and I am committed to guiding those souls who are struggling with addictions. Addictions come in many flavors. The most common on the earth plane is addiction to mind altering substances. But there are many other addictions that can interfere with a developing soul. These include abuse addiction and addiction to self-destruction. Souls who gravitate to an addiction are there on earth to rid their hearts of anger. Now, this anger is not the obvious anger most humans associate with the word, where a person becomes abusive verbally and many times physically. No, this anger is deep seeded. The soul has been injured through many lifetimes and harbors the injury deep in its heart. The soul must remove this anger to continue its soul development. Remember, all souls are in the process of removing the heavy elements in their hearts to move closer to God. God is always pleased to see the efforts so many souls put forth because of their love for Him. The struggle to succeed many times is difficult. We archangels and angels intercede as much as we can to guide these souls to success on their chosen paths.

Now, this may all sound very heavy and abstract to you so let me give you a few examples. I, together with several angels and archangels worked with a soul who decided to incarnate to earth to free its heart of a deep seeded anger and self-pity. This anger, which occurred many times to this soul over several incarnations, was directed against those in positions of authority. After much counseling with the Masters, the soul came to us for preparation to incarnate with the intent to experience and remove this anger. When the soul chose to return to the earth plane, we all knew it would to be a very difficult life for this soul.

The soul requested another soul to journey with it. This second soul was an experienced soul and agreed to help. The two souls were welcomed into a very loving, kind and happy family. All the elements the struggling soul needed to be exposed to for success were in place. The little boy and little girl were the first children for this family. The parents had a lot of love and support from their extended families when the babies arrived. Again, the environment was very conducive to give this little girl the basic training/guidelines to traverse a difficult life. As the twins grew in age, they developed a very close relationship. We watched this development hoping the little girl would always remember to reach out to her brother when needed.

The children were introduced to the existence of angels at a very young age. They loved their guardian angels and were always thrilled when they saw a picture or statue of an angel. The little girl developed a deep love for her guardian angel and would always greet her guardian angel each morning when she awoke. Both she and her brother would talk to each other about their guardian angels.

As the twins started school, the little girl was starting to feel inferior to her brother. The teachers always compared them to each other with an extra comment on how well her brother looked, or how well-prepared his lessons were, or how well he succeeded in track or swimming. She started to resent her teachers and ultimately her brother. She kept her feelings to herself for many years, but the anger and self-pity were growing slowly. She wanted to escape but her family's love for her was strong enough to keep her straight during these formative years. Finally, the children went their separate ways to college. They attended different schools. The young girl was very happy with this separation for a few months but then became very lonely – she missed her brother tremendously. She thought about the times when she resented his popularity and how they were compared to each other. She remembered the hurtful feelings in her heart and how she wanted to run far away from him so she could become her own person. Well, she had that opportunity right now. After several weeks of feeling sorry for herself because she was alone without the support of her brother, she went for a long walk in the park nearby. She walked aimlessly along feeling depressed and lost. She passed joggers and walkers whom she recognized from school. They all just nodded and kept on going. One jogger, whom she recognized from a chemistry class, stopped and asked if she was okay. The young girl looked up with tearful eyes and said yes, thank you. The jogger stayed with her and said she didn't look okay and asked if she would like to talk. They stopped at a nearby bench and the young girl burst into tears. She told the jogger how lonely and depressed she was and how guilty she felt for resenting and disliking her twin brother and had wished so hard for them to be separated that it had really happened. She didn't know what to do now; she didn't know how to untangle all her bad thoughts. The jogger listened, and was truly concerned. When the young girl finished talking, the jogger asked if she would like to join her and a few friends at a local diner. She said it would be company to get her mind off herself. The young girl joined the group and found them to be very open and friendly. One young man in the group asked if she would join him for a smoke outside. She responded that she didn't smoke but would be happy to join him. She recognized the smell of the smoke immediately when he lit the cigarette. It was an illegal drug and she immediately returned to the diner. He followed and told her she should try one to help calm her nerves when she gets upset with herself. She turned and glared at him believing he was pushing the drug on her and also trying to control her. She politely said goodbye to all and left the diner. Now she was angry again but her anger had shifted from herself to the young man with the drugs. 'How dare he assume I needed calming down', she thought. She decided her life was as it should be and she didn't need others to intercede and tell her what to do or how to do it.

She returned home for the summer following her first year of college. When her brother walked through the door, she ran to give him a big hug. Whoa, he said, how did I deserve this? I thought you were happy to be rid of me, he laughingly said as he pulled her hair. She told him she liked being on her own but had to admit she really did miss him. They stood and smiled at each other. They each were busy that summer catching up with their friends, but were able to spend time together. Her brother noticed his sister was different. He saw her personality changing. She seemed to take some of his teasing as attacks and become very defensive and then argumentative. Other times, he noticed she was extremely calm and somewhat forgetful. She also looked like she had lost some weight. Being away from Mom's good cooking would do that he rationalized. But what about the extreme personality changes he had observed. What was causing these changes in his sister? He decided to investigate.

He watched her carefully now, pretending to tease her as usual. When she reacted calmly, he looked into her eyes. They seemed to be glazed over. This was an alert signal to him. Then he watched the triggers that caused her to become argumentative. They seemed to come from statements she could perceive to be downgrading to her or sometimes authoritative. He approached her one afternoon on a jovial note asking if she remembered how they always stopped when they saw an angel picture or angel statue; how in love they were with the angels. She shook her head yes and added she hadn't seen any angels since she left for college. He asked her if she still talked to them. She said no. He asked, 'why not'? She said she just never thought about it. She continued saying she believed the angels are for children and babies. As a child grows up, the child outgrows the angels. We are on our own now, she said. I believe you're wrong, he responded. He watched as she stiffened, ready for an attack. He then smiled, put his arm around her and said, 'listen, Sis, we have been together a long time and I guarantee the angels are always with us but you have to talk to them. They love to hear you call for them. You look a little stressed since you have been home but I bet if you talk with your guardian angels you will see that life is not really difficult'. She looked at him hesitantly and asked if he still talked with his angels. He answered yes, everyday. She then just stared at him. What am I missing, she thought, are angels the path to happiness and success?

They both continued on at college and graduated with honors. He graduated with a degree in history and continued studies in archeology. She also graduated with a degree in history but decided to enlist in the military. She always had strong feelings for her country and wanted to be a major force in assisting her country against the perceived enemy at that time. When her brother heard the news of her enlistment, he called her immediately. He knew she did not handle authority very well and until she progressed through the officer ranks, she would be taking a lot of orders. He told her she still had time to change her mind, she could move to a more peace serving organization to help her country. He truly feared her reaction to authority could get her court-martialed. He closed the conversation by reminding her to talk to her angels every day especially to help get her through officer training. She appreciated and yet resented his call. She thought he still did not believe she could succeed. She felt she needed to surpass him in position, stature, and earnings. The seed from their childhood competitions was still churning in her heart.

The first three weeks of officer training were grueling both physically and mentally. The orders to perform were swirling all around her but the need to survive the physical demands gave little time for her to react mentally. As the training slowed towards the end, the orders were still being barked but she now had time to absorb and react to them. Anger was building in her heart to the officers above her. She succeeded and graduated from the officer training school with distinction and several awards. Her parents and brother came for the graduation ceremony and celebration. They were very proud of her and for the first time in many years, she felt she was important to her family.

When her brother had the opportunity, he pulled her aside and told her how very proud he was of her accomplishments and asked if she had started talking to her angels. She felt joy in her heart that her twin brother was truly proud of her but told him that she was still not talking to her angels. Why, she asked, why is this so important to you? He responded that she had just chosen a very dangerous and difficult profession and she needed all the help and protection she could get. She thought he was crazy. She was being prepared very well so why did she need the angels, she asked. You will see, he answered.

During her first year as an officer, the young girl encountered many controlling officers above her. She could not disagree with their orders or she might face military discipline. She remembered how she handled stress in college and decided to try prescription drugs to keep her personality in check. They were easy to get from the doctors and her life became more manageable. She received a promotion within two years and was responsible for several people but she reported to a very strong female officer. The two of them did not get along. They seemed to be in constant competition. Her new boss was beautiful, well liked, and extremely successful. This brought back memories to the young girl who always felt she was in competition with her brother. To try to outperform her boss, the young girl stayed on the job until nine to ten o'clock at night and returned at six o'clock in the morning. She became obsessed with this routine. She needed to outperform her boss and she needed a way to handle her boss's authoritative personality. Her life pattern continued like this for almost a year; depriving herself of sleep, of a social life, and calming herself down with drugs. She liked her life because she believed she was winning. She believed she was winning the war in her heart against authority. She was going to stamp it out forever if she could destroy the authority figures above her. Her drive to succeed intensified. She lost a significant amount of weight, which she was proud of because she felt she was thinner than her boss. She looked haggard from her work schedule, but she believed no one could beat her if she worked this hard. She was becoming consumed with her work ethic and her need to surpass authoritarian suppression.

Her brother visited her about eight months into her new position and was shocked when he saw his sister. What are you doing to yourself, he asked. She had no idea what he was referring to. She said she was just working hard to succeed. He told her that her behavior was not necessary. He said she was intelligent and strong enough to defend her position on any major decision or controversy. Why did she have to attack authority, he asked. Authority is needed to lead. You are a leader, he said. She responded saying that she did not perceive herself as a leader. She needed to prove her ability to lead to herself; she believed she needed to overthrow authority. 'Sis, where are you coming from', he responded. You don't belong in this environment with feelings like that in your heart, he said. Look for the angels, talk to them, you need them now, he said. He asked if he could help her in any way, and she responded, yea, I need your angels, I think mine went back to heaven for reassignment.

The young woman continued on and made no changes to her lifestyle. She continued with her self-inflicted abuse believing she was starting to succeed. Her boss recommended her for a new position, which carried a higher rank. She succeeded, she thought, I am moving on, I am being recognized. The new position required the young woman to transfer to a troubled area in the world to oversee over one hundred troops. Before she could assume command and move to the area of combat, she was required to undergo a full physical. With the results of her blood work came the shocking news that she was too weak to travel and take responsibility for the lives of others in a combat zone. She had succeeded and now she felt defeated again. She was admitted to the hospital where they immediately put her on IV's full of nutrients for her malnourished and dehydrated body. She immediately felt trapped and the anger against authority started to rise in her heart. This is a conspiracy, she thought. It was her previous boss who orchestrated this. She remembered her boss asking her if she was ill and advised her to see a doctor many times. She did this to me, she stated aloud. A young doctor quietly stood at the door of her hospital room and asked her whom she thought injured her body to this degree. She just stared at him wanting to be away from anyone whom she thought would want to control her life. He sat in the chair by the bed and stared back at her. As she looked him squarely in the eyes, she suddenly felt an overwhelming feeling of peace. His eyes are so kind, he can't be all that bad, she thought. No, he answered to her thought, I'm really not bad and you must start believing you are the only one who controls your life. WHAT, she said, how did you know what I was thinking. I know all your thoughts, he answered. That is impossible, she retorted. I have only known of the power of angels and they can hear thoughts. That is correct, he answered. Soooo, she said slowly, are you an angel? He bowed his head slightly and quietly said yes. I am your guardian angel. What is your name, guardian angel, she said sarcastically. Pelantes, he responded. And what have I done to deserve a visit from a real angel, she asked. Well, for starters, you have just about destroyed your body with your obsessive behavior. I am NOT obsessive, she retorted. So, Pelantes said softly, please describe the behavior that caused you to be hospitalized. I was just doing my job, she said, it was very demanding and I wanted to succeed. Succeed at what, responded Pelantes. MY JOB, she shouted. But didn't you receive many accolades from your superiors acknowledging your success? Well, yes, she whispered, but you don't understand. Please tell me what I don't understand, said Pelantes. This is a long story and I would say you don't have time to listen because I'm sure you have other humans to look in on. No, he said, right now it is all about you. Well, I don't believe there is much to talk about; I had a demanding, and high-powered job and I did not want to fail. Fail at what, he asked. The JOB, she shouted. A nurse walking past her room heard her shouting and immediately came to see if the young girl was hurt or in pain. What is wrong, the nurse asked. The young girl looked up, startled, and pointed to the chair Pelantes was sitting in. It is his fault, she said. Who, the nurse asked looking at the empty chair. Whoever made you upset has made a quick exit, the nurse stated. She asked again if the young girl needed anything and when she shook her head 'no', the nurse left the room. The young girl looked back at the chair expecting to see Pelantes but he was gone. Great, she thought, now I just scared my guardian angel away. Well, who knows if he really is my guardian angel. I never called for him, anyway, so why would he just materialize like that. I must have been hallucinating with all the drugs I'm taking, she thought.

She was very weak and slept a lot. Several days after she was admitted to the hospital, her brother was standing by her bed when she awoke. Hey, broth, what are you doing here? Why didn't you call me, he asked. Look at you; I can't believe you did this to yourself. Do what to myself, she asked. Your obsessive behavior has almost killed you and you are not out of the woods yet, he said sternly. But I did get promoted and will be overseeing over one hundred troops. That is significant, she said. Yes, it is, but you are not there yet. Think, sis, tell me why you felt compelled to do this to yourself. You must remember that when you move into new positions, the demands will be greater and you will have even stronger personalities to deal with. As you climb the ladder in the military or any corporate ladder in life, each step gets more difficult and thus more demanding and authority figures abound for every decision you make. You have to be strong for this lifestyle and not retreat into yourself and beat yourself up to prove to others you are as good or better than they. I know you have never accepted any type of criticism from any authority figure. I saw that when we were kids in elementary school. I wanted to help you but you always pushed me away. She was very tired now from listening to her brother. Tears rolled down her face and she asked to be alone now with her thoughts. As he walked out the door, her brother said softly but sternly she must cleanse her heart of these negative authoritarian feelings before she could begin to heal her body.

Her body healed slowly and shortly after being discharged from the hospital she asked for a medical leave from the military. She thought about her brother's visit as well as her guardian angel's visit. What was I doing, she thought, that an angel would actually come visit me. But then, was it really an angel? She decided it was a dream but she could remember Pelantes words now as though he just said them. Both Pelantes and her brother were giving her the same message – that she was destroying her body in response to her negative feelings against authority. My brother is right, she thought, I would have difficulty in my new position. She knew whom she would report to but felt she could handle it because she just survived her previous boss. But did she really, she thought as she pondered over her brother's words of handling stress by destroying her body. She walked many miles each day sifting through all the comments given to her by many in the hospital. They may be right, but I only did what I did to survive the environment, she rationalized.

She returned to the military to assume her new position. Unfortunately, another candidate filled that post. She was then put in line for the next available opening that matched her qualifications. She was starting to get very angry now, feeling authority put her down again. Her obsessive behavior patterns slipped back into her life. We angels were watching her very carefully now because she had not yet cleansed her heart of the negative feelings against authority and her body would not be strong enough to survive another obsessive abuse pattern. We sent signals and messages to her brother to visit his sister. Pelantes decided to take on the human form again to help the young girl see herself. Her brother visited for a weekend and by the third day he saw she was slipping into obsessive behavior. He then looked closer and saw she had lost weight since they were last together and he found a new prescription bottle on the counter. It saddened him to see this happening again and decided to gently introduce the subject of her behavior so she wouldn't run from him. What is happening in your life, he asked quietly. Nothing, she responded, except I am in a holding pattern at the office until a new slot opens for me. He decided not to address her problem directly, and asked if they could get together more often as they did when they were younger. He felt he could build a trust between them and hopefully get her to lean on him and talk when she felt she was having a bad day with her superiors. She agreed hesitantly because she thought her brother just wanted to keep tabs on her. He called her everyday and she answered his questions but was growing tired of his 'spying' techniques. He asked her to dinner frequently carefully watching her eating habits. He knew he had to keep her strong. This continued until she received her new assignment. She was again assigned troop duty but not in a war-torn area. It was an important assignment and she was selected from a group of five candidates. Her brother pointed this out to her emphasizing her skills and personality as a leader. His goal was to try to get his sister to see herself as a strong and fair-minded leader. He decided to discuss the relationship she had with her previous boss…how she felt persecuted and how she almost destroyed her body because she would not be open-minded to the leaders above her. He reminded her that the officers who selected her believed she truly was open-minded and fair and could lead as well as be led by those in authority above her. These words stung, as she had never considered herself open-minded and well liked by others.

The new assignment was very difficult as the young officer met with orders from above as well as being challenged from officers below her rank. Self-doubt, self-pity and anger rose once again in her heart. Her obsessive habits returned again. She needed to succeed. Pelantes entered her office one afternoon but she did not recognize him. She did not like being interrupted like this and showed her impatience immediately. Pelantes spoke quietly and slowly. Why are you doing this to yourself, he asked. WHAT, she said. Who are you? You have no right to march in here and make that kind of statement. Please leave or I will have you thrown out. Look at yourself, he said. She was about to call for help when she looked into his eyes. She immediately calmed down. What are you doing here and what are you doing in a uniform, she asked. I do what I have to do when my earthly charges are destroying their bodies and moving away from God. I am here to show you what you are doing to yourself and offer my assistance to guide you back to your written path here on earth. What written path, she asked. I don't remember writing a book about myself. It is a spiritual book of your life here on earth. I have no idea what you are talking about, she retorted. Now, if you will leave, I have a lot of work to attend to. I will leave you now but I will always be with you. My parting words are for you to look inside your heart, see your anger for authority, and remove that anger. Don't die with anger in your heart. She watched him walk out the door with no idea of what he was talking about.

She excelled in her combat position for several years and collapsed one day in her office. The years of striving to overachieve had finally caught up with her. When her brother walked into the hospital room, he put his arms around her and with tears in his eyes asked why she did this to herself. She whispered she needed to succeed; she needed to surpass authority. He asked her if she still had anger in her heart. She shook her head no. How did you overcome it, he asked. She told him her guardian angel came to her and talked to her about her anger. She thought about it for a very long time, she said. After much soul searching and reconnecting with her guardian angels and all the angels, she finally saw the pain and anger in her heart. She told her brother it was a long journey but she believed she finally succeeded. But look at yourself, he exclaimed. Why did you let this happen to you? It was a very hard process, she said, and I continued to beat my body up while I was working on my soul. I am very happy now, she whispered. I feel I can go home to heaven. With tears running down his cheeks, he kissed his sister good-bye, told her he was very proud of her and that he would miss her.

There was much jubilation here in heaven when she returned. We all went to meet this spirit. Pelantes opened his arms to receive the soul and she stood for a moment basking in his love, smiled and said 'thank you for working so hard to save my soul'. She looked at me and the other archangels and thanked us for preparing her so well. The area then became quiet as God entered in all His glory, opened His arms to her, smiled, and said 'Welcome Home'.

ARIENTELLE

HELLO, MY NAME IS ARIENTELLE. I am with the corps of angels who work with spirits preparing them for the earth plane as well as receiving their tired souls when they return back to heaven. Souls may choose to face extreme difficulties on the earth plane. These difficulties range from abuse, traumas from mental and physical violence, to severe and debilitating illnesses. I help prepare these spirits by reviewing all that is involved on the earth plane with the path they may choose. I show them the choices they will face and emphasize the key areas that can take them away from their written plan. These choices are open to the spirit's free will. I teach them how to be strong when the world may be collapsing around them. And above all, I tell them constantly to remember to call on the angels to help them succeed.

Why do spirits choose to experience a difficult life on earth? Many spirits are working very hard to advance their souls to be closer to God. It is a stepwise progression. By choosing a very difficult time on the earth plane, the spirit is learning a lot spiritually even if it does not realize it while in the human form. Taking a horrible experience, accepting it with love and then reaching out to help others who are also suffering is a significant learning experience for a soul. The most difficult aspect for the soul then is recognizing and accepting the difficulties that are written in its life plan.

I would like to tell you about two special spirits I worked with recently. The first spirit wanted to experience a large amount of difficulty on the earth plane. He was a very lively and ambitious spirit and was determined to advance his soul as high as he could on this one return to earth. The great Masters and many archangels counseled him to reduce his workload. He was determined to write it all in his life plan. He had great enthusiasm and truly believed he was strong enough to take on a difficult life. He was advised again to reduce the abuse he had written but even over here, spirits have free will and he chose to keep everything as it was written.

The spirit placed itself in a hardship the moment he incarnated to earth. His mother was sad when she realized she was having a baby. This was her first child and she didn't know what to do. She was not sure who the child's father was and was frightened to return home. She had left her family to explore the world. She felt she could not return, announce she was pregnant without knowing the whereabouts of the father. This would destroy her mother and father whom she knew loved her very much. She did not want to hurt them with this news. She got a menial job during her pregnancy knowing she would run out of the money she previously earned from working the street scene.

Her baby was born with no complications except he had no home. His mother left him at the hospital as soon as she was able to slip out. The little boy received a lot of attention from the hospital staff and the news channels. Everyone was looking for the mother, but she was nowhere to be found. The child was placed in a foster home until a possible permanent home could be found. Everyone's heart went out to this little abandoned baby. The nightly news question was 'how could anyone abandon a newborn baby'?

As time passed in his first foster home, it was noticed the child was not extremely alert. Following medical tests, it was determined the child was partially blind. This reduced his chances of moving to a permanent home soon because more tests were needed to determine the possible cause of this type of blindness. The child remained in foster homes for many years. Many of the homes were very loving and caring to the young child and worked to help him with his level of blindness. When he needed new glasses or eye medications, many of the foster parents used their own money to help the child.

Unfortunately, a few of the homes he transitioned into, left him by himself for many hours at a time. He was uncared for, alone and frightened. But even at his young age, he knew somehow he would be moved to another home. The experiences in these various foster homes left many scars in his heart. By the time he was ten years old, he felt he had enough abuse and tried to run away. He had no idea where he was going or how to survive but he had to try to find a better way of life. The authorities always found him and returned him to the foster home environment.

He continued in school until he could stand it no longer. His reduced eyesight made learning a struggle and the taunts and harsh words from his classmates hurt him tremendously. They talked about him having no parents; they called him coke-bottle eyes, and they jeered at him when he tried out for the swim team. Nobody likes me, he always thought. Why? What have I done to these people? I am so lonely, he said to himself one day. Why was I born? I am an awkward, ugly duckling, he thought of himself.

He left school and the home he was living in when he was sixteen years old. The family never seemed to like him from the day he arrived. He could see the love these parents gave to their biological children but always pushed him away when he tried to give them a hug. He cried many times at night before he went to sleep. They won't miss me, and they will probably be glad that I am gone, he reasoned. The young boy had saved enough money to exist for a few months. He hopped a train with the intent of going to a bigger city where he believed he could blend in even with his disabilities. He fell asleep on the train, missed his destination and continued to a small seaside village. He had never been to the ocean and was intrigued to see the huge body of water and the numerous boats at the dock. The dock seemed to be a very important area for this town because he saw many people pushing and hollering when each boat arrived loaded with all kinds of fish. He moved to a secluded area to watch with interest all the transactions occurring around each boat. It was exciting to watch. Suddenly, he decided he wanted to be a part of all this action. His eyesight was poor and he was small in stature but surely there was something he could do to be a part of all this activity. I am not stupid, he thought, I could learn to work on the boats, to catch the fish and handle the nets. Yes, he decided, this is for me. This is where I want to live.

The young boy wandered around to get the 'feel' of the town. Many of the local people living there looked at him suspiciously. There were always many strangers in the town but they usually had business in the dock area. He wandered aimlessly into a café. After ordering, he asked the staff person who to contact to get a job on one of the boats or at the dock. The waitress directed him to the dock manager but added the young boy didn't look very seaworthy to qualify for that type of work. He ignored her comment, determined all the more to succeed in something in life.

He walked back down to the dock area and stood in a doorway looking at a very big, scruffy, middle-aged man. The young boy must have looked terrified because a passing worker whispered 'don't let him scare you, he's a good guy if he likes you'. The young boy continued to stand there until the dock manager looked up and bellowed to the young boy to come in and sit down. The young boy sat in a straight chair silently for about five minutes trying very hard to hide his shaking hands. Suddenly, the office became very quiet and the dock manager turned and quietly asked the young boy what kind of job he was looking for. The young boy looked up, surprised that the manager knew he wanted a job. The manager read his face and said that news travels fast in a small town. The manager then evaluated the young boy, his stature, his poor eyesight, and asked for a reason for his interest in dock work. The manager told him the work he was looking for was hard labor and required long hours unloading the cargo from fishing boats. By the time the boats come back to this dock, he said, they are full of all kinds of fish. To unload this kind of cargo, he continued, you need to be strong and sure-footed to lift the fish-filled containers and swab the slippery deck. The young boy truly believed he could perform. He wanted to prove to someone that he could succeed especially after being jeered and pushed around so much in high school. This was a big task for a small guy but he wanted to tackle it. The dock manager saw the enthusiasm in the young boy's eyes and told him to report to the dock at 5am the following day. The young boy jumped out of the chair with joy, shook the manager's hand and ran out to the street. He returned to the café and asked the waitress where he could get a room because he just got a job. The waitress smiled, gave him some addresses that rent rooms, and congratulated the boy. But in her heart she knew it was going to be very tough for him. She just hoped he would be able to endure the rough life he was about to enter.

The young boy was on the dock and ready to work before 5am. He looked around at the stillness. There was no one in sight, no boats coming in or going out. He saw 6am, 7am, 8am, and still there was no one. He was getting worried and questioned himself if he heard the dock manager correctly. He looked out on the horizon and saw a large fishing boat headed his way. Why so late, he wondered. Then he heard the sound of cars approaching and heavy footsteps on the dock. He turned around to see a large number of workers descending on the dock. They walked directly to the slip where the approaching boat would anchor. He observed that they all came together and they all knew the time the first boat would arrive. Should I follow them, he thought. No, he decided, they don't know me and I really don't know what to do. He decided to go to the manager's office. The door was open so he walked in. The manager was talking on the phone and ignored the young boy. The boy sat in a nearby chair and waited patiently. The manager knew he was there but chose to ignore him. The manager interacted with several other workers who came to his office but refused to even look at the boy. Why does this always happen to me, he thought. This is just like school and my foster homes; people just ignore me. Am I invisible? The boy then cleared his throat a few times to try to get the manager to look at him. Nothing. Well, he thought, two can play this game. I am just going to sit in this chair and wait. As long as he is in here, I am too, he decided. So the young boy sat and sat. At 4pm, the dock manager stood up, looked past the young boy and walked out. He did not shut the door so the young boy continued to sit. Soon, the dock became very quiet again. The boats were unloaded, cleaned and back out to sea. The young boy was very hurt and questioned if he should move on. No, he said aloud. I can play this game; I will not give up. He walked to the café and the waitress could see the disappointment in the boy's eyes. Several of the workers told her of the boy's first day on the job. She wanted to give him some encouraging words but knew these words would travel back to the dock. She could lose her job. She smiled at the young boy when she brought his food and asked if he had a good day. He shrugged his shoulders and said 'yea'.

Since the door to the manager's office was left open, the young boy decided to sleep in the office. He wanted to greet the dock manager as soon as he returned in the morning. The night was early yet so the young boy wandered around the office looking at the papers scattered around the desk and chairs. He was not interested in anything in particular. He was just passing time. He wanted to stay in the office and not wander onto the deck area for fear a cleaning person would close and lock the door.

He heard a car pull into the area about midnight. He had already turned off the lights. He heard footsteps coming towards the office so he hurriedly hid behind a large leather chair. The men slammed into the room with determination. He heard some of their comments against the dock manager. They believed he was skimming money for himself and cheating them by using unbalanced scales. They ransacked his office looking for some particular papers but the young boy could not understand the name of the documents they were looking for. He stayed as still as he could, terrified to breathe. He heard a comment that the dock should be torched but several others said no because they wanted to catch the manager red-handed in the act of cheating. As they were leaving, he moved a little to watch them walk out the door.

One of the men looked back and saw the young boy's shadow. He hollered to the others to come back. They sauntered up to the chair and swiftly pushed it aside. And who are you they growled at the young boy. He stood up sheepishly and kept his eyes down. He was afraid to look at them.

As the young boy lay unconscious in the hospital, everyone wondered who he was and where he came from. He had no identification on him. The gang of men beat him badly and left him on the floor of the dock. The dock manager found him early in the morning. The young boy's guardian angels hovered over him while he lay on the dock. They whispered many messages to him to be strong, not to give up. They kept repeating to him that they were there to help him hold on to his life. As he slowly regained consciousness in the hospital, he kept saying the name Arientelle. His guardian angels stepped aside as Arientelle entered the room. A tall, very strong looking man looked at the young boy and said I am Arientelle. I am here to help you. The young boy put on his glasses and said thank you but I don't know you. You know me from a long time ago and you have forgotten, Arientelle replied. Arrangements have been made for your recovery but you must put aside your wounds and hatred from your past, repair your body and move on with your life here on earth. You still have many difficulties to experience. Talk to your angels; tell them to help you. Listen for their messages. With that Arientelle walked out the door.

The young man spent many more years on the earth plane. The incident on the dock left him crippled, in need of a wheelchair, and a heart empty of love. He experienced other tragedies that challenged him even more. He was attacked and robbed several times, and his wheelchair was stolen. As he aged he became very bitter at the world around him. His angels never left him but he refused to talk to them, to hear their voices, to see their signs. As he sat one day in the park, feeling sorry for himself, a young man came and sat on the bench next to him. The crippled old man did not look up when the stranger sat down. The young man looked at the old man and said 'it looks like you've had a pretty rough life, old man'. With that, the old man shot back 'you have no idea'. Well, the young man said, did you ever ask your angels for help? The old man looked at the young man and said that is the dumbest statement he had ever heard. How in the world could angels have saved me from all the misery and mishaps I've encountered in my life, the old man said. They would have helped you through the difficult times, the young man retorted. Angels help you understand what you are experiencing in life. When you know this, it is easier to accept tragedies and difficulties knowing you are advancing your soul. Soul, schmole, I am too old for all this stuff, the old man grumbled. I have no idea about this soul stuff and these angel things you talk about, he said. I will just die soon and that will be the end of this miserable time I've had on earth.

The young man ignored these comments and proceeded to tell the old man he definitely did not want to die with so much misery and hate in his heart. The young man started to prod the old man about what he knew about God and love and happiness. The old man fought back many times but the young man would not give in to the man's refusal to open his heart to hear about God. The young man found a soft spot in the old man's heart when he mentioned how the dock manager saved his life. The old man countered that the dock manager was the cause of the beating but the young man said 'no'. The young man reminded the old man it was his choice to stay in the manager's office that night. Think about it, old man, you received several signs and messages from your angels that night but you chose to ignore them. The waitress at the restaurant told you to be careful, to stay inside at night. One of the tenants where you had your room asked you to come over to visit. And while you were in the manager's office, you kept having a feeling you should get out of there. They were all signs and messages from your angels. Think about it, the young man said. Angels have always been in your life. They are always there for you but you need to pay attention and let them into your heart. They bring you messages of love from God. The young man got up to leave. The old man sat with his head down. What is your name, he asked. I am called Arientelle. The old man looked up suddenly upon hearing that name but the young man was gone.

The old man often thought of that day in the park. He thought about angels and God. He heard many people make comments about angels, God and love. He decided one day to research them. He proceeded to read many books and would sit for hours thinking how this could all be possible. He started to make little comments to his angels to see what would happen. To his surprise, he found himself smiling more and seeing the people around him as truly good people. Gradually, he realized more people were smiling at him, talking to him and they were truly interested in being around him. Maybe I'm not a bad person, he thought. I like the feeling of belonging. I like the feeling of being loved. Maybe there is something to this angel stuff, he thought.

The old man lived several more years in his beat-up condition. He worked cautiously with the angels always waiting to be rejected, to be pushed out, to be jeered, and even to be injured again. He returned to us peacefully, surrounded by the few friends he made in the latter part of his life. His guardian angels stood with him until I entered to take his battered spirit and help him heal. He recognized me as soon as I entered and thanked me for coming to him when he was most desperate. He said he believed he was a failure. The struggles on earth were overwhelming just as you warned they would be, he said softly. I comforted him and told him he was a great success. In all that you experienced, you did open your soul to God's love and messages while still on the earth plane. God, in all His glory, then walked in to welcome the soul back home. He knew the soul was battered so He took the soul into His arms and filled him with love.

The second special spirit I recently worked with chose to experience some very unique difficulties. This spirit is a very experienced soul having traveled to the earth plane many times. The spirit had previously completed several difficult lifetimes on earth and requested to return to continue her soul development. Because of her previous experiences, this spirit was very receptive to our advice on critiquing her life plan. We felt the spirit was ready to return to earth. I reminded the spirit to remember the angels.

The spirit incarnated as a healthy baby girl. Her parents very happily received her. She was the only child born to the couple and they showered her with love and a bountiful life. Her mother taught her to always say good morning and good night to her guardian angels. The little girl loved being around her parents and always wanted to please them in any way she could. The three developed a strong bond among themselves. If one was sad for any reason, the other two felt the sadness and tried to bring happiness into the household.

This went on for several years. Together, they all enjoyed life to the fullest.

One day, the child's mother came home from a doctor's visit and went straight to her bedroom. The little girl couldn't understand why her mother and father wouldn't let her into the bedroom. Her father finally came out and told the little girl her mother was very sick. The little girl exclaimed she needed to see her mother right away to make her better. When she finally was allowed into the bedroom, she climbed onto the bed and snuggled right up to her mother. The little girl saw her mother was in a lot of pain. I can rub your tummy to make it better, she whispered to her mother. Her mother smiled at the child and said, yes, please, that would be nice. The two lay there together for several hours. The little girl held her father's hand walking out of the bedroom asking when her mother would come and play with her again.

Her mother returned to us later that night. We knew this would be traumatic for both the father and daughter so we sent many angels to comfort them. It was a very difficult transition for the father and daughter to be two instead of three. The little girl tried to be strong for her father because he was so sad. She looked at the guardian angel picture in her room every night and asked the angels why did they take her mother to heaven. She never got an answer and as she grew older she sometimes wondered if angels really existed.

The little girl was growing into a beautiful young lady. She traveled extensively with her father who seemed very happy when his daughter accompanied him on these trips. The young girl became very ill shortly after returning home from a trip with her father to a foreign country. She entered the hospital for extensive tests since her illness was not easy to diagnose. She had horrific pain in her body. Her father had flashes of his wife's illness and had great fear for his daughter. She had learned to be strong for her father because she loved him so much and did not want to see him sad. The diagnosis was a rare liver disease she contracted while traveling with her father. This was similar to her mother's illness and both feared she would die shortly.

The young girl agreed to try an experimental drug. Because of her age, it was believed the drug could be beneficial to her. She was still in high school and expected to graduate in the spring. Her father was extremely despondent and this gave her the determination to live. She stayed in the hospital for her treatments and was able to keep up with her studies with the help of her friends and teachers. However, her father was becoming very depressed which was affecting his health. He was losing weight and suddenly seemed very frail. This worried the young girl for without her father, she would have no one. Her father left the earth plane peacefully shortly after she was released from the hospital.

The young girl made many friends in college. Despite her frailness from the liver disease, she always rallied to support her friends with any project they became involved in. She was unable to participate in many physical activities but that didn't stop her from cheering her friends. They all loved her spirit and enthusiasm. Her friends awarded her a trophy for top cheerleader of their group at the end of her second year in college. She was very happy at this time in her life. She was moving past her illness and the loss of her parents. She questioned God many times why this happened to her. She believed she was a good person. She worked very hard to stay positive and not be angry with God but sometimes that was very difficult.

Midway through her junior year in college, she contracted a virus that caused her to be hospitalized. This depressed her again, and she continued to ask God to please tell her why all these difficulties keep happening to her. She was totally frustrated with life. Her friends stayed very close to her during this hospital stay. They saw for the first time how very sad she was. They felt it was their duty to cheer her and bring her happiness. She loved it when they came to visit her.

She truly felt their love. On the day she was to be released from the hospital, several of her friends arrived to take her to her apartment. She was happy to see them and happy to be going home. But something was wrong. She could see it in their eyes; hear it in their voices. So before she left the room she asked them directly what was wrong. Something has happened, I can feel it, she said. Tell me before we leave here. They all put their eyes down because there were tears rolling down their cheeks. There was a terrible accident, they said quietly, and two from our group have been seriously injured. O My God, she echoed as she fell into a nearby chair. What happened? Are they alive? What hospital are they in? They were biking on the mountain trail and a truck came too close to them and caused them to crash into a ravine, one of her friends responded. The truck stopped and called for help immediately and that is probably why they are alive. They are pretty banged up. When the young girl heard her friends were being treated in the hospital she was about to leave, she insisted on visiting them. I am strong enough and I want to see them and talk to them. I must cheer them, she said.

The young girl continued her studies at the university and graduated with honors. She celebrated with her friends and shortly thereafter they parted, each to follow their own path in life. The young girl was extremely lonely but had learned how to be alone. She secured a position in a large teaching hospital upon getting a graduate degree in occupational therapy. She loved to help people and make them smile especially when they were so despondent due to their reduced bodily skills. The young therapist excelled in her work. She soon was recognized and applauded for not only helping patients regain their everyday ability to dress and feed themselves but also for her talent to lift their spirits. She was happy deciding this was her reason for existing. Her thoughts were now turning back to God. She finally forgave Him for taking her parents from her at an early age and for her weakened immune system. She realized all her past events prepared her for this present position. Many of her patients were young and angry. They believed they were invincible and wanted her to restore their bodies to be one hundred percent normal. Most of the time she knew this was impossible and worked to open their eyes and have them accept their new way of life.

One day, a young patient came in and asked the young therapist if she worked with angels. The young therapist looked up quickly at the mention of angels because this brought in a flood of memories of her mother who loved the angels. The therapist shook her head no and asked why the young patient asked this question. The patient responded the special work she did with her patients in helping them understand and accept their injuries was truly the work of angels. The patient said she believed the angels were working through the therapist. The young therapist looked the patient directly in her eyes and saw an enormous amount of peace and love. She also felt a surge of love enter her body with chills going down her spine. I never thought about angels in my work, she responded to the patient. You should, the patient responded, because you are glowing with their love right now. Talk to the angels, the patient said; bring them into your life. I know you have been sick recently but it was the angels who helped you through that and many previous illnesses. The young therapist excused herself for a moment and when she returned the patient was gone.

She thought about this patient for many months trying to figure out why she gave her the angel information. Sure, she was getting sick more often, but she had learned to not become despondent over her frail body but she started to question God again. She had helped so many people over the last several years. Why does God keep putting me in the hospital, taking me away from helping people, she thought many times. And what should I do with this angel stuff? I know my mother loved the angels, she thought, but that was her belief, not mine. She had a wonderful life only to die at an early age. I can't figure out how believing and working with the angels brought her any consolation when she lay dying. But, I do remember her smiling right before she passed away and telling me to stay with the angels. What did she mean, the young girl thought. She returned to work and continued helping her patients physically and spiritually. She also put aside any thoughts of the angels when they came to her.

Shortly after her encounter with the patient who talked about angels, the young therapist was diagnosed with pancreatic cancer. She was devastated by the news. She tried to stay positive and keep a smile on her face, but her patients knew something was wrong. When several patients learned about her illness and prognosis, they rallied together to help her smile just as she helped them to smile. The patient who talked about angels walked into her office one day, sat down and smiled at the young girl. So, tell me, the patient said softly, are you talking to the angels yet? The young girl did not hear the patient come into the office and spun around in her chair when she heard the voice. No, she responded, and I don't intend to. What are they going to do for me now, she asked. I will die in a few months anyway. I know that, the patient responded. You are still bitter and angry about your past, your parents dying, your medical problems and now your terminal cancer. But you have hidden and even buried your anger to the point that no one ever knew how sad you truly feel. Look deeply into your heart. You wanted happiness but you were not open to receiving it. Instead you poured all your energy into making everyone around you happy. This was a cover-up for you. You found you could smile a little when you helped others smile. So, the young therapist responded, what is wrong with that? Nothing, in fact it is admirable but you have neglected yourself in spreading all this cheer. Just once, we wanted you to scream and come to us with your broken heart and tell us all your hurts and sorrows. You have carried a huge burden inside you for many years. Your angels have always surrounded you just as your mother told you. Through the years they have sent you many messages of love and support but you refused to listen. I don't believe in angels, the young girl responded. In fact, right now I'm not so sure about God. I've tried to stay positive about Him but I keep getting hit with one catastrophe after another. I see many of my friends sailing through life successful in a career, marriage, and children. I ask myself over and over, why me? I love my career and I feel successful in that I am truly helping people with their physical struggles. But other than that, I feel a failure because I spend most of my free time trying to stay well. How can I have any meaningful relationship? How could I get married and have children? I feel cheated. Bravo - the patient in her office exclaimed. The young girl looked perplexed but then became irritated. What do mean by that, she said loudly. The patient said lovingly she was happy to see the young girl finally express the feelings that were hidden deep inside her heart. They just slipped out, she said with tears in her eyes. The patient walked to the young therapist and put his arm around her shoulders and whispered she was surrounded by love, surrounded by angels. Let them into your heart and let the healing begin. Who are you, the young girl asked with tears running down her cheeks? My name is Arientelle, the patient responded and quietly left the young therapist's office.

The young therapist continued with her career for several more months. During that time she recalled in detail the visit by this person called Arientelle. By thinking and searching deeply, as Arientelle suggested, she was able to see herself grow spiritually. She looked into her heart and remembered the hurt she experienced after each traumatic event in her life. She looked deeply and saw how she buried the pain. As she grew weaker from her cancer, she grew stronger spiritually. She remembered her mother's dying words to her, 'remember the angels'. Her mother had whispered, 'the angels love you just as I love you; stay with them, receive their love'. She remembered not wanting to hear about the angels because she did not want her mother to die. Then her father became ill and died also. She remembered her thoughts again. Where were the angels her mother talked about? Where was this love she was supposed to experience? She thought about it and decided the angels were not around her and not helping her with all her pain. She decided at her father's funeral to walk away from the angels. Her thoughts at this time associated angels with the loss of her parents. As she searched even deeper in her heart, she saw her loneliness and sadness increasing but she didn't want anyone to know. She believed they would feel sorry for her so she put on her clown's mask.

Her journey to spiritual recovery took many months. It was not easy for the young girl to look at her soul so critically. It was painful because she did not want to admit to herself that she truly missed being a part of the love that is available to everyone. She did not want to admit that she purposefully rejected the angels' love. She realized now their love was coming from God. She searched very hard to understand her own health issues. I believe I am a good person, she said many times to herself, so why has God sent me so many illnesses to overcome?

As she lay in the hospital undergoing another chemo session for her cancer, Arientelle walked into her room. The young girl was sleeping lightly and opened her eyes when she heard footsteps. She recognized Arientelle and asked why he came to the hospital. Arientelle smiled and spoke softly. We know you are still struggling with sorting out your life experiences. Listen to what I have to say. You contracted the same virus that caused your mother's death. She died because the doctors did not fully understand the virus and did not know how to treat her. Since then much research has been successful in understanding and treating this virus but not in removing it from the human body. You have provided the doctors and researchers with much needed information about this virus because you were mentally strong enough to survive this many years after being diagnosed. You are a strong soul and despite all the physical suffering you have experienced, we want you to know you are surrounded by love spiritually. It is all yours if you just reach out and welcome the angels into your heart. There are many people here on earth who love you also. Welcome them into your heart. You have spent your entire life helping others, now it is time to let them help you. Arientelle walked over to the young girl, kissed her lightly on her forehead, then walked to the door to welcome many of the young girl's college friends and patients. As they streamed into the room, they brought gifts, cards and banners rich with 'thank you' messages for all the care she gave them. With tears streaming down her cheeks, the young girl searched the group for Arientelle, but he was gone.

The young girl returned to us shortly after reuniting with her friends and patients. All were very sad to see her leave the earth plane at such an early age. But there was great jubilation here in heaven. Her guardian angels walked with her on her journey over here. She was happy to return and very happy to see me again. Her soul beamed with light and happiness when we reviewed her success on the earth plane. It was very difficult, she stated, even more difficult than I ever imagined before I incarnated. Thank you, Arientelle. I needed to be successful and you were always there to help me. Thank you also, dear Guardian Angels, and I apologize for pushing you aside in my life. With that, a great light descended on us as God walked in, extended His arms and welcomed her back home.

CHAMUEL

I AM ARCHANGEL CHAMUEL. I have been to the earth plane many times and I am always impressed with how hard humans try to have God as a part of their lives. There are many places of worship and humans pride themselves on attending services and honoring God. What I also see is the learning deficit that occurs at these services. Those in charge of the services work very hard to communicate God's love on the earth plane but the majority of people attending these services don't absorb or relate to the information about God at the services. Also, many do not understand what is being said to them about God because the lecturer has forgotten to relate God to everyday life in this century. The earth is not in the first or even tenth century, it is in the twenty-first century. Humans cannot relate to a nomadic life as portrayed in many religions. This is the digital age. Humans relate to speed…flying around the world in a day, instant communication via the Internet and visiting with family members separated by oceans by using the computer with visual technology. Yes, the world has advanced significantly since Jesus, Mohammed, Elijah, Buddha and many other great Masters walked and taught on the earth plane. Their messages are timeless but must be made relevant to this century so all humans can understand and reap the benefits of their teachings about how to understand God and live their life with Him.

A theology instructor at a university struggled with his lectures about God in modern society. He had difficulty transferring an ancient lifestyle to a modern lifestyle. Most of his students knew how to skip class and take his tests because he never challenged their thinking. The students just memorized the chapters, passed the tests and received an easy A for the course. I watched the instructor year after year present this type of class and saw many students shrug their shoulders when asked what the class was all about. We sent many angels to this instructor advising him how to make his class more relevant and meaningful for the students, how to show them that God exists today as strongly as he is portrayed in the early writings. There was much about life and God they could learn in this class. Many students would be moving on to positions of authority and power. This class had the potential to truly anchor them with God so they could handle powerful positions and the politics that come with dishonesty and backstabbing.

Angel Ione was proud of her earthly godchild. He was extremely intelligent, personable and loved by all who met him. While at this university where he studied law, he decided to take a course in theology. Although he had already taken the required ethics course, he thought the theology course might be helpful in his career so that he might view people as human beings instead of a court number. After three classes, he was extremely disappointed. This class did not meet his expectations. He wasn't interested in the tribal names and lifestyles of the early people who roamed the earth listening to different teachers who came to teach them about the love of God. The young man approached the instructor after class one day and challenged him to relate the information in this class to modern day living, technology, and the populations of today's world. Ione was working with the young man, advising him of the challenges life presents and how this theology class could be a stepping-stone in preparing young adults for life after graduation. The professor was both startled and offended by this young man. He actually felt threatened because he had been teaching this course for six years and was well versed with its theological contents. He was proud of his knowledge. He was proud he could identify any date, nomadic group, area of the world with the prophets at that time. The young man acknowledged the professor's scholastic ability but stressed he was in this class to learn the teachings of the prophets and how he could relate them to his life and prepare him for the future. The professor relaxed once he understood the young man's motivation to help him open his eyes to what he was really teaching. The professor continued teaching his class for this semester as he had previously but met several days a week with the young law student for some very intense and sometimes heated discussions about the presence of God in today's world. The young man grew spiritually while working with the professor and felt he developed a stronger set of values for his life.

Ione was with the young lawyer as he progressed in his career. He joined a law office that offered a variety of specialties. He worked with small and large contracts, wills, divorces, and estate settlements. He stayed with the law firm for several years working to gain experience before he set out on his own. The young man would stop at a pub many times on his way home from work. He would often engage in conversation with many different professionals who frequented the pub. Within a few months he was swept into believing he would be a good candidate to run for a government position. This was exciting to him and he believed he could win and be a strong voice for those he represented. He won this and many more elections and started to climb the political ladder. He was happy and truly believed he was making life a little easier for the general public.

As he climbed higher in the political realm, he saw a lot of corruption occurring behind the scenes. This made him a little nervous but he vowed to himself to be strong and stay aware of what surrounded him. Ione was watching him carefully, standing always by his side but the young lawyer had stopped talking to her many years previously. He was becoming ever more popular and relying more on assistants relative to the details of his work. He believed he was always making the right decisions in his positions but many times the crowds and the glamour blinded him. He continued on this course for several years falling deeper and deeper into the palms of the manipulators so prevalent in the political arena. He climbed to the top of the political realm and thought he could rule the world. So many political analysts, news reporters, aides, friends and even enemies surrounded him that he had very little time to himself.

With all this success, he rarely looked to God. He was too busy. When reports came to him of people struggling to survive because of unemployment, increased cost of living, or the increasing casualties of a senseless war, he passed the reports to an assistant to resolve the problems. Political analysts, enemies and even some of his friends started to criticize his cold-hearted behavior. He ignored negative reviews and commentaries, believing he was above reproach. He believed he was performing well in his position because he was so popular. He believed the negative statements were due to jealousy. He also believed no one could do this job as well as he.

Then the cries began to come from everywhere to remove him from office. The lawyer still didn't flinch. There is no way this could happen. He believed the public still loved him as they did early in his career. He received a letter during this tumultuous time from a professor at his alma mater. At first he did not recognize the professor's name but remembered the theology class mentioned in the letter. The professor wrote asking if the young man remembered any of their conversations about the presence of God in today's world. The professor emphasized in the letter how adamant the young man was at that time in demanding the professor equate the presence of God in ancient times with the presence of God today. The professor related that he had changed his curriculum but he hadn't seen the young man incorporate God in his life as they discussed. The professor reminded the young man that he had taken his theology course to build a stronger character to be able to always stand strong, make the right decisions and always keep God in his heart. You were a champion for people, their needs, and their rights. What happened, the professor wrote, when did you close your heart to God? If God were truly in your heart, you would not be as you are now. God does not treat people as you have treated them in your career. We discussed this many times, do your remember? I listened and I learned a lot from you that semester you were in my class. I hope you keep this letter to remind you to bring God into your heart and stand strong among all the negative forces surrounding you.

The young man sat and stared at the professor's letter for a long period of time. He left his office and started walking.

Ione walked with him sending him messages of love from God. He could not hear her. He had turned away from God many years ago believing he was strong enough now to face life head on without the aid of God. He believed he had prepared himself with God in his younger years that he could now walk the earth plane alone. His heart was heavy as he recalled the many discussions with his professor. He was trying very hard to rationalize his behavior in light of all that was placed in his heart in the theology class. He could not see that he was wrong, that he was hurting people. Ione and I discussed what we could do to bring this man back to God, to open his heart to God and the angels. He sat on a park bench and began to reread the professor's letter. I came and sat next to him. He did not look up. I could see he was very troubled and hurt. I asked him if he would like to talk because he looked so upset. He shook his head no and then I saw a tear in his eye. I held out my hand for comfort and told him I was Chamuel Archangel. He still sat there apparently reviewing his life and what he had become. I was quiet for several minutes when he looked up suddenly and almost shouted my name. An archangel, he said, what have I done so drastically wrong that an archangel has to come to me? Aren't I assigned just a guardian angel and where has she been through all this? How could she let me slip away from God so much?

The young man and I sat there for several hours discussing how strong he was with God at the university and how he let his ego start ruling his life, eliminating his need for God or any celestial being. Through his ego he believed he could live a full, happy life and rise above all negative distractions. I told him that is exactly why he needed God in his life. Without the help of God, the negative forces in life were able to enter his psyche and become a part of him. He asked exactly what I meant by negative forces. I told him the forces were greed, selfishness, self-centeredness, believing others are here for him and not vice versa. I reminded him these were the elements many of the great Masters talked about in ancient times that he discussed with the professor. Yet look at your life, I said, it is just like the lives described in the ancient teachings. You are living for yourself while you are in a great position to help thousands of people in the world live a better life. You have much influence, use it wisely, I said. The young man responded that he did not understand. What is wrong with accepting gifts from individuals or companies if I am truly trying to help them, he asked. Nothing is wrong, Chamuel replied, if what they want is not detrimental to the public. Most of your monetary success has been working with those who have the money to buy their success through you. You listened and you enjoyed the vacations, the exclusive travel arrangements, and notoriety. You were blinded. Then there were the cover-ups. Do you remember, I asked. He looked at me blankly just as he did during many inquisitions to his actions. You claimed you did not remember many events that were extremely unethical or knowing that they occurred and you denied your involvement. These are all negative forces that exist in the world and will readily seek you out once you drop your guard. You moved away from God and the angels, His messengers. You were swept up in this lifestyle and with your power to rule. You were sent many, many signs to look at yourself, evaluate your actions. Ione, your guardian angel, directed the professor's letter to you in an effort to awake you. She consulted with me many times about how far away from God you were drifting. She believed that with angelic help, you would come back to God. You have a strong background with God and a strong set of morals that are especially needed for this high profile position you now hold.

Ione stood behind the young man with tears in her eyes as he asked how he could rectify all his wrongdoings. Was it too late, he asked. I told him it is never too late to get reacquainted with God. He will be angry with me and besides I don't know if I am strong enough to change, he said. Everything will come crashing down on my family and me, he cried. How can I handle that? I am in too deep; it is easier to stay, he quietly stated. Ione and I looked at each other with disbelief. He was so close to returning to God. We saw fear starting to encompass him. I looked him straight in the eye and told him fear was another great negative force and he just opened the door and let it in. He didn't believe me because he said he needed to protect his family from widespread scrutiny and criticism. He said this was a moral obligation. I agreed with him but told him that with our help and guidance he could walk through the legal trials, verbal and written attacks, and return to the person everyone loved and believed in when he was first elected. It will be a long and bumpy road, I advised him. You have to take steps now before you begin the process to check yourself every day to ensure you are not slipping back into those negative forces. Start by going back to your university and visiting your theology professor. He will help rekindle your love for God and strengthen your inner core to take the steps needed to stand up to those companies and individuals who were a part of your downfall in public office and with God. Learn to listen to your heart, hear the voices of your angels; they are whispering God's messages to you. Be aware of the signs they send you. It could be a message on a billboard, a song that you hear several times, conversations you might overhear that pertain to a problem you are currently working on. We are all around you. Open your eyes; pay attention to what you are seeing and hearing. We will be working very hard to help you but it is up to you to choose to be with us or stay as you are.

The young man sat quietly now for several minutes. You have just thrown the book at me, he exclaimed as he slowly raised his head. I saw the tears in his eyes. Yes, I want to be a good person. I loved my life and how I felt about myself when I was in college and even when I first entered politics. I am very afraid right now, he said. I don't know if I am strong enough to right all my wrongdoings. He stood slowly, turned his head to look into my eyes and then quickly walked away mumbling he had a meeting to attend.

Ione and I continued to walk with the young politician but he ignored all of our messages. He continued in his political position for several more years, sinking deeper into corruption. He totally turned away from helping others when there was nothing in it for him. His family saw what he had become and walked away from him saying he was a different person. They did not know him any more. When the trials finally came for corruption and scandalous behavior, he still believed he was above the law. He was not and Ione and I watched with sorrow as his perceived empire came tumbling down. The last remarks from the judge stated that he knew this man when he was a young lawyer and politician. The judge stated that the politician was a good man, a just man. He looked directly at the politician and said he was very sorry to see a good, promising, intelligent person be reduced to nothing.

The university professor followed the demise of his former student closely. He decided to visit the incarcerated politician. The professor looked at the politician and asked why he hardened his heart when so many of their discussions focused on the importance of keeping God in one's life. The politician was silent for several minutes. The professor sat patiently. The politician shook his bent head and said he didn't know how this all happened. The politician said he believed God was always there even in his bad days but never thought about it. The professor told him that God was definitely there but he chose to ignore Him. Come on, the professor said; remember our discussions, even arguments about the presence of God and the angels in our lives. You were so strong, so adamant in your beliefs that I didn't think you would ever close your heart to God. You had the potential to be a great leader, a humanitarian leader that would be accepted by the world. You really blew it, the professor said, and just for the love of money, power and fame. Let me tell you this before I leave…God is still with you, and there are many angels trying to deliver God's messages to you, just as they always have from ancient times to modern times. Wake up and listen to them while you still have a chance here on the earth plane. As the professor rose to leave, the politician whispered thank you.

It took many months of deep thinking before the politician decided to change his heart. He thought deeply about our conversation in the park and his conversation with the professor. Slowly, he started to look for signs from the angels. He remembered he was very good at recognizing them when he was in school. We sent him many signs and watched how he progressed in recognizing them and more importantly responding to them. When he was ready, we sent messages to his heart. He did not hear us for several months, but as his heart started to open to God he received our messages very clearly. His life in this negative environment slowly changed. He recognized what was happening and started to feel good about himself again. It was a long time since his heart was this content and happy. He began to look at his fellow inmates and the prison guards differently. He previously believed they were all against him. He now understood this was his own paranoia. As he grew back to God, he reached out to help those around him. In the beginning, he just listened to those who were lonely, who needed a shoulder to lean on. He made an effort to be kind to the prison guards, knowing this was their job and a very difficult job because of the verbal abuse they received daily.

The lawyer/politician left the prison environment a changed man. He knew his career as a politician and as a lawyer was over. However, he felt confident he would be directed to a new career. He waited and watched for signs and messages from the angels. He knew they would come. He saw an article about his university in a magazine and felt the angels were telling him to visit his professor. Upon walking through the door of the theology department, the professor looked up and with a great smile said, 'welcome back'. The lawyer thanked the professor for all his efforts to bring him back to God, and move him out of his corrupt life. As they talked, the professor asked the lawyer if he would like to help him with his theology course. The lawyer looked puzzled. He reminded the professor that he was a lawyer and not a theologian. The professor stated he had many lawyers and other professionals take his course for the same reason he had…to strengthen their morality and ethics in order to withstand the negative forces so prevalent in life.

The lawyer recognized this offer was from the angels and immediately accepted. He grew in his love for God and the angels. The class grew in size and popularity because together the professor and the lawyer were able to bring God, the angels and the messages from the great Masters of ancient civilizations to the twenty-first century.

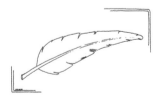

MARTICUSE

HELLO, I WOULD LIKE TO introduce myself to you. My name is Marticuse and I am with the realm of angels who help those souls who choose to return to the earth plane because they were not able to complete their life's plan on a previous incarnation. There are many reasons why this can happen. As you know, life on the earth plane can be very difficult because there are many challenges that cross your path, all strong enough to pull you away from your written plan and sometimes keep you from returning to it. Some of these challenges include drug abuse, a selfish or violent lifestyle and anger. I know all of you can see how these challenges can interrupt a soul's journey on earth but there are other detours in life that can interrupt your journey a lot more discreetly. Some examples include suicide, illness, physical impairments and injuries, poverty and excess wealth. We help educate souls who have returned to us by helping them understand why and how their decisions caused them to move away from their written life plan and ultimately away from God.

I have worked with many souls who ended their time on earth because they became overwhelmed by the complexities of life. As we reviewed their life with them, we showed them how we tried to interact with them and help them through a difficulty they were experiencing at a particular time. We showed them our signs and messages that were continually sent to them. We educated them again on their use of free will and how we angels respect and honor their choices. Following these life reviews, many souls were then able to understand that they were not strong enough to return to the earth plane when they did but they exercised free will and returned with the belief they would succeed.

We work very hard to impress on all the souls who return to us the enormous amount of spiritual help that surrounds them on the earth plane. We teach them to just call on us when they are feeling distraught, angry, unloved and lonely. Our work is intense because we want to impress this information onto their souls so they will remember us when the separation veil falls. We help them choose an environment on earth conducive to educating them about God and us angels in their early years. With that said, let's follow a few souls to show you some challenges on earth, how they are a part of life and how they can interfere with a soul's life plan.

One soul who worked with us returned to the earth plane with our approval and love. She was born into a family of moderate means with several siblings. Her parents taught all their children at a young age to say 'hello' every morning to their guardian angel and to God. They were told this would always bring them happiness and love for that day. The little girl and her siblings were given the freedom to continue onto college after high school or to venture out into the business world. The young girl was the only one of her siblings who chose not to go to college. She was bored in many of her high school classes and couldn't wait to graduate and see the world.

We were very happy for her because she was still talking to us and learned to listen for our messages and look for our signs. We watched her carefully now because she would have some difficult decisions to make to stay on her life's path. She remained with her parents for about a year after securing a job in the large city nearby. She made friends easily but didn't look at their friendship very closely. Her sister tried to tell her to be careful of some of her friends because she could see they were shallow and manipulative. The young girl told her sister she would be okay. She said she felt they needed her to help them at this time in their lives. Her sister warned her again but knew she would not abandon her domineering friends. The young girl was having fun working, partying, and doing group outings.

She continued with her lifestyle until one day she saw one of her friends get arrested for stealing. The police arrested the young girl as an accomplice even though she had no idea her friend was taking anything when they were together in the department store. She was incredibly frightened in the police car. Her friend looked at her with contempt and told her it was her fault she got caught. The young girl had no idea how to respond to that accusation. She was incredibly hurt. She thought this was her friend. She was ready to defend her but her friend was ready to cast the blame on her and let her go to jail. We surrounded her at this time, sending her many messages and signs. She was completely closed to us. Her parents were very strong and supportive of the young girl. They believed every word she said as she described the incident to them. Her sister walked in, looked at her and asked if she remembered her warnings. The young girl shook her head yes and added she did not believe her sister at the time.

The young girl's parents convinced their daughter to stay at home for a while longer and to change employment to the town in which they lived. They now knew how easily influenced their daughter was with stronger personalities. They felt they needed to protect her for as long as possible. However, they knew their daughter could not stay with them forever and they could not keep danger away from her. Her mother would casually tell her many times to talk to her angels as she did when she was a child. The young girl reconnected with us and happily received our signs and messages. She returned to the happy soul we knew before she incarnated to the earth plane.

But time marched on, and the young girl wanted to get out into the world again. She wanted to experience all that she could in life. She had saved enough money to take an extended leave of absence from work. She wanted to 'see the world'. Her family was very worried but her mother kissed her goodbye and whispered, 'remember the angels'. She decided to sail to as many countries as her money would allow. She met two friends on her first sailing voyage and felt them to be good and honorable. They had fun on their first excursion in a foreign country. However, they met several local people about their age who told them to meet them at a restaurant the following evening. They looked forward to going to this restaurant except when they saw its location. It was located in a sparsely populated area of town. It frightened them and they considered turning around. Then they saw several expensive cars drive by so they all confirmed to each other it was probably okay, so they continued on. The address they were given was in a broken down warehouse building. Now they were really frightened. Before they could turn around and run, a car came up behind them and two men pulled them into the car. Their hands were immediately tied and their mouths were taped. The car sped away and drove around for several hours. The young girl had no idea what these men wanted because there was no talking between them in the car. When the car finally stopped, the young girl and her two friends were pushed out the door and left by the side of the road. They lay there, stunned for several minutes. They proceeded to untie their hands and remove the tape on their faces. It was a very dark and desolate area. As they stumbled around, they tripped over something large. It scared them, so they started walking along the side of the road not knowing where they were or where they were going.

The police picked them up the next day as they were resting on a park bench. The police accused them of being part of a notorious gang well known in that part of the country. The police told them they found enough evidence to arrest them for the fatal injury of a local townsperson. The girls protested but the police took them immediately to the police station. The young girl was dumbfounded. How could this happen, she kept asking herself. Due to the evidence the police had against them, they were quickly tried, convicted and placed in jail. She and her friends were unable to send any messages to their families. Her family did not expect her back home for several months so they were not too concerned about the lack of communication from their daughter.

The young girl was becoming very despondent. She tried repeatedly to explain her innocence to those with whom she came in contact with in the prison. We were very alarmed with her state of mind because we did not want her to choose suicide and end her commitment to this lifetime as she had done previously. We sent her many messages but they were always returned to us. Her heart was closed. It was imperative we contact her. As she lay on her bed one afternoon, a cleaning lady stopped at her cell and asked if she could cheer her up because she looked so sad. I am sad she responded. I am wrongfully accused of a horrible crime and I just can't communicate to anyone that I am innocent. The young girl kept her eyes closed while talking to the cleaning lady believing she would not believe her and would go on about her cleaning duties. The cleaning lady stayed and asked the young girl if she ever talked to her angels about this situation. Opening one eye, the girl shook her head no and said why should she. They can see me, she said sarcastically, they know where I am. And why haven't they told my parents? No, she said, the angels only seem to be around when everything is going well for a person. How in the world did you come up with that idea, the cleaning lady asked. Well, it's true, the young girl said; look at me now. Why didn't they come to my trial? Why didn't they bring in anyone to help me? Did you ever ask them, the cleaning lady said. By now, the young girl was sitting on the side of her bed, staring at the lady with the broom. The cleaning lady looked very tired and worn out but she had a very beautiful face, the young girl thought. Did you ever ask them to come to your trial, to guide you with your statements to the jury? Again, the young girl shook her head no. I guess it's too late she said softly. The cleaning lady told her in a strong voice that it is never too late to contact the angels. They are already here but you must be open to them. You must welcome them into your heart. They have been sending you messages every day to try to help you but the messages are falling on deaf ears and blind eyes. You are sitting here day in and day out feeling sorry for yourself. Have you decided how you are going to end your life? The young girl fell back on her bed with that statement. What are you talking about, how did you know? It is obvious, with your body language, lack of communication with me as well as the others you have met in here. Don't do it, the cleaning lady said. Your main purpose here on earth is soul development. If you remove yourself from this world, you stop your soul development process. Who are you, the young girl shouted. I don't want to hear all this stuff about the soul and staying on earth. This is my body and I control whether I want to stay here or not. DON'T DO IT, the cleaning lady said firmly. With that she picked up her broom and proceeded down the hallway. She shouted back to the girl, 'if you need me, just call out my name – Marticuse.

The young girl sat on her bed for what seemed an eternity. Who was that lady, she asked herself over and over. The thought of calling on the angels as she did as a child seemed preposterous to her. But she kept thinking about the angels a little more each day. Finally, she whispered ever so faintly to her guardian angels to please come and help her. She asked them to come quickly because she still intended to remove herself from this world because she believed that was the only way she was going to get out of this jail. All the angels were joyous with this little whisper. We now have a chance to save her from her dark thoughts. They sent her many messages of love, trying to move her into a more positive frame of mind. She must feel love, they said, to survive. One morning, she awoke to find a feather lying on the floor next to her shoes. She just stared at the feather remembering it was a sign from her angels telling her they were present with her. She began to cry but they were tears of happiness and not despair.

After serving two months in jail, the young girl and her friend were released. They were stunned and speechless. What happened, they asked the warden when he came to personally release them. He said there were several more crimes of that nature committed but one person survived and was able to identify the attackers. Investigation of this crime and all the previous ones including the one the girls were accused of, found the notorious gang was responsible. The girls were free to leave. The warden advised them to be extremely careful in their future travels.

As the girls walked through a nearby park discussing their experiences in the jail and deciding what to do with their lives now, a tired looking old lady with a beautiful face walked toward them on the path. As she came closer, the young girl looked at the old lady directly and exclaimed, Marticuse! The old lady stopped, smiled and put her arms around the young girl whispering she was very proud of her decision to stay on earth and continue developing her soul. Looking into the old woman's eyes, the young girl saw only love. She thanked her for saving her life and for bringing her back to God and His angels.

I worked long and hard with another spirit who came to us wanting to return to the earth plane as quickly as possible because it did not have complete success in its previous life. This spirit was strong and was angry for falling into some of the traps that crossed its path. The spirit was determined to study and remember as best it could all the obstacles that exist to slow soul development. The spirit kept insisting to us it was ready to return. We would then again show the spirit the difficulties it had in its previous life and how it continued to walk farther and farther from what it wanted to accomplish. This quieted the spirit enough for us to fully prepare this spirit and it was elated when we nodded positively to present the plan to the great Masters for the final sign-off for its incarnation to the earth plane.

The soul entered the earth with great fanfare. The little baby girl was showered with love, and happiness because this soul was born into a well-respected and well-known family. The parents had delayed starting a family to further their political careers. The child was endowed with the best of everything including schools, travel, a mansion to live in, as well as a nanny. The parents absolutely adored the child, but they returned to their busy political careers in the first year of the child's life. They claimed to be affiliated with a religion because they felt this was necessary to be accepted in their career fields. However, they never introduced their little girl to God or His angels. The girl's nanny observed this omission of God in the child's life and asked the parents if she may talk about the angels to the little girl. The parents said yes because they felt this was no threat to their careers.

The nanny talked constantly about the angels to the infant girl. The nanny believed the infant understood her at another level because she always smiled and cooed when she heard the word angel. The nanny continued her angel stories and bought many angel books and pictures for the little girl. By the time she was three years old, the little girl told her nanny the name of her guardian angel. The nanny was very impressed and happy. The little girl proudly said her guardian angel's name was Sogenie. Every day thereafter, the nanny asked the little girl if she said hello to Sogenie and she watched silently as the little girl appeared to be talking to her guardian angel. The nanny would smile as she said to herself, 'I am setting the groundwork for her to have help if she ever needs it later in life'.

The little girl grew into a beautiful, intelligent and well educated young lady. She was very popular among her peers and was always well received by strangers. She seemed to have a magical aura around her. People loved to be around her because she had so much energy and determination to succeed. Following college, she fell into step with her parents and government politics. They were very happy to see their daughter take such an active role in the community and country. Her charismatic personality and enthusiasm acted like a magnet drawing large crowds to hear her speak for a local cause. She loved the attention and sometimes seemed to thrive on it. Her nanny followed her progress and political success. She was very happy for the young lady and always whispered a little prayer to the angels to give her extra protection for she was now truly entering the fast lane of success in life.

As her public life expanded, she met many good, kind-hearted and hard working people as well as the not so good. She learned to receive the jeering comments from the skeptical and was always able to counter with answers to sway them to her way of thinking. She was very proud of herself for this talent. She met and talked with them after her speeches telling them she could use their high-spirited thinking and energy in her campaigns. Several readily signed on with her. She also met many high level influential people who were interested in her ability to inspire crowds as she did. They wanted her to be a part of their organizations or to be a part of their political agenda. However, many of these influential people did not have her best interests in mind. Several saw they could use her for their self-advancement.

In her busy schedule, there were always lunches or dinners with both good and bad top level business people. All intended to recruit the young lady to advance either their organization or a worthy cause for humanity. They donated large amounts of money to her selected charities. They also wrote large checks for her personal use when she supported their requests. She previously investigated these requests to ensure they were all legal, but as her schedule intensified, she did not have the time for this research. Since she trusted many of these people she relaxed the investigative requirements for contributions. The word quickly traveled among the unsavory ones and in a short period they knew they could easily buy her support in the political realm.

The young lady had many employees monitoring and dispersing financial aid to hundreds of charities. She also had a large number of employees working with her politically. As her popularity grew, so did her partying and drinking. She loved to have non-business get-togethers with high-ranking officials. She felt it was a release from the stress of her political career. Many felt they were 'in' when asked to one of her house parties. As time progressed, the number of parties and the number of guests increased. The young lady rehired her former nanny to help her with these parties. The nanny accepted immediately looking forward to being with someone she loved and nurtured as a child. However, after the first party, the nanny just cried. Her lovely little child had grown into a very selfish, self-centered person. It broke her heart to see the level of alcohol she consumed and was shocked when there was evidence of illegal drugs being used. She left her first party and never returned. She refused any contact with the young lady. She kept questioning herself as to where she had failed being her nanny. She believed she had instilled a strong moral character and a strong knowledge of the angels. She definitely needs the angels right now, the nanny thought sadly. She is going down the wrong path in life. So the nanny wrote the word 'Sogenie' on a piece of paper and mailed it to the young lady's home address.

As time moved on, the young woman's organization and political career became increasingly corrupt. She paid little attention to political groups calling for an investigation of her personal contributions to charities and an investigation into her personal life and tax statements. She believed she was above all this. She believed since she was so charismatic and everyone was so impressed with her, she could end all the inquiries. She loved her lifestyle and was not going to let intruders take it away from her. She pretended to cooperate with the legal requests because she knew how to sway the attackers to her side. At least she thought she could. There were several very strong people on the investigative boards who refused to fall for her persuasive tactics. The allegations included money being taken from the charitable contributions sent to her organization and her receiving large amounts of campaign money for personal use. The young woman was not going to be taken apart and criticized. She believed she was a good person remembering her college days when everyone loved her. So the young woman decided to destroy business and personal records. As she was working late one evening, she found a sealed envelope on the corner of her desk. She opened it slowly being very skeptical because it was typewritten with no return address. As she unfolded the paper, she stared at the word printed in the middle – Sogenie. She had no idea what it meant and tossed it to the side and continued destroying her files.

We watched very closely now as this soul had wandered very far from her intended path on earth. She had placed herself in a great position to help a lot of people not only in her country but also around the world. However, she chose to follow many of the detours that crossed her path as she progressed through life. We were sending her many messages now knowing it would be extremely difficult for her to find her way back to her life's path without our help. This was why she returned to the earth plane. Her goal was to help as many people as she possibly could in her lifetime. She did not want to do anything else except help others.

When she did not recognize her guardian angel's name on the paper from her nanny, we decided to send her stronger signs to open her mind to our help. However, she did not see or hear our signs and messages. One sign was blatant. The license plate on the car in front of her at a red light read 'ANGELS'. There was absolutely no response as she stared at the license plate. When she was standing in line at a grocery store, the girls in front of her were talking about knowing the names of their guardian angels. Again, there was no response as she stood there and listened to the conversation. We inspired her nanny to send another note to the young woman. The nanny wrote the words, 'Sogenie is the name of your guardian angel'. She personally delivered it to the young woman and told her, as she handed her the envelope, 'read this because only God can help you now'.

The young woman tried very hard to remember her guardian angel, Sogenie. We continued to send her messages. The investigation was getting intense and ugly. The goal was to topple her from her pedestal and make her responsible for her wrongdoings. She maintained a strong and stoic presence when she was required to appear before the court. One day, a prosecutor asked her how could she have the appearance of an angel and be so dishonest. These were the words she needed to hear. We sent her a picture of an angel in her mind. She held on to the thought and looked at the prosecutor with tears in her eyes. Suddenly she saw herself talking as a young child to her guardian angel named Sogenie. She closed her eyes and whispered softly to us, 'please help me'. There was great jubilation here in heaven. She was now ready to work with us.

The judge was not lenient with his sentencing. 'Restitution must be made to all those you injured' he bellowed. She gladly accepted her punishment and a chance to turn her life around. She worked very hard for the remainder of her time on earth and was successful in completing her intended task of assisting as many people as she possibly could. She talked to Sogenie several times a day always thanking her, welcoming her into her life and asking for guidance. The young woman renewed her friendship with her nanny thanking her for bringing her back to Sogenie and thus saving her life.

AHNTARIO

My name is Ahntario and I am with the realm of archangels. I work with the angels who receive the spirits who choose to return to the earth plane solely to help other souls with the many difficulties and crossroads human life presents. These spirits have traversed the earth plane many, many times to develop their own souls. They are now at a level of soul maturity to return to the earth plane and recognize life's challenges in order to assist others who are unable to see the many choices available on the earth plane. However, these spirits also have free will when they return and can choose the wrong paths in life that may ultimately affect them and their friends and families. So this is a very delicate life plan for a spirit to choose because they know they are strong enough to succeed but they also know they can fall prey to the many traps life presents.

The training the angels present for these spirits is intense. Angels review the life plan the spirit has written and show the spirit all the possible detours it may encounter once it returns to the earth. They stress the need for the soul to stay in contact with them so when difficulties appear, the soul will automatically call for the angels' assistance. I teach these spirits the power of the archangels and the importance of maintaining a relationship with us. I show the spirits how the angels call on our assistance to help guide a soul out of a difficult situation or to provide an extra layer of protection when needed. These spirits prepare with us archangels and angels and wait patiently until we approve that they are ready so they can advance for review before the great Masters.

Let me tell you about two spirits who chose this life plan. The first spirit had a strong personality and was very experienced having traveled and successfully completing many life plans. This spirit led previous lives involving some difficult plans that included addictions, physical and mental handicaps, jealousy and anger, hatred, and greed. This spirit had successful as well as unsuccessful life plans but was always determined to advance her soul. So it was with great fanfare and jubilation over here when this spirit was ready to incarnate to the earth plane with the intent of helping other souls with their own soul plans.

The family welcomed the beautiful baby girl with total love. She was the second child for this couple and they were very happy to have a little sister for their son. The parents believed in God and taught the children many stories about God and His angels. The brother and sister grew very close to each other and together they would talk to their angels, giggling and smiling when the angels were present. When the little boy was sent off to school, the little girl was deeply saddened. She was alone and thought her brother was being punished. He was a very active child, always running, refusing to listen to his parents or grandparents. His activity caused them to raise their voices many times and send him to his room until he calmed down. His temper would rise as he stamped off and slammed his bedroom door. When he returned home that first school day, she jumped up and down and tried to hug him. She was so happy he returned home.

The parents loved their little boy but were becoming exasperated with his conduct. He seemed to be filled with anger and with this anger came frustration. In contrast, the little girl was extremely calm and peaceful. She was a joy to be around. When the parents sent their little boy to his room, they would unwind by holding the little girl in their arms. She seemed to exude peace and love. They often wondered how their children could be so different having the same biological parents and ancestry and living in the same environment. The little girl loved this attention but felt guilty she was not sharing it with her bother. She would ask her parents if her brother could join them. They usually said no and explained to her he needed to learn to control his behavior. At this time in her life, she did not understand what they were saying and felt sad she could not share this attention with her brother.

By the time the little girl was in fourth grade, her brother was in seventh grade. His behavior and language outbursts were constantly getting him into trouble. His parents were very concerned about their son. They were called to the school many times to discuss his behavior. There were also days when he did not go to school. The parents were shocked the first time the school officials gave them this information. Where did he go, what is he doing, they asked each other. When told of his absenteeism, the parents knew the boy was truly troubled and sought professional help. The boy resisted, as was his nature but the parents were successful in getting him to attend a few sessions with the doctor. When he returned home after these sessions, he would immediately go to his room. His sister always asked to join him. He loved to be around her because of her peacefulness. She never asked how the session went, and never asked why he had to go. At her young age, she only saw that he needed to feel love. She knew her parents loved him, but she saw they did not show him their love. She would go into his room and talk about anything and nothing to him. She loved this time with him, she loved giving him her love and helping him calm down.

The parents were able to get their son through high school without any major incidents. They felt a great relief for this and gladly sent him off to college. They then had three years to enjoy their beautiful daughter. The young girl felt lonely without her brother and worried about him. She talked to us angels every day to watch over him. We were happy to see her staying connected with us especially when she saw that someone needed guidance or protection. She was moving along her own life plan very well. At school, there were several girls she saw who were constantly bullied. She watched the bullying for several weeks and then felt compelled to step in. She stood up to the attackers and challenged them to come after her. She stood alone facing three females. Both her voice and body language were extremely strong. The three girls turned away and yelled she was next. This was the beginning of her career as a champion of the underdog. Word spread quickly in school and on face-book and soon she was held high on a pedestal as a true hero. She felt very happy to help her school friends. She did not think of herself as a hero at this time but she did enjoy the attention.

She graduated from high school with high honors and recognition for helping others. Her brother was very proud of his little sister for all her accomplishments. They had many talks during this time. She asked him about his temper and outbursts of frustration. He lowered his head and said quietly he was still struggling. He lost several friends and was very sad when they went away. They told him he needed to get his temper under control before he did something disastrous to himself or to another person. The young girl looked lovingly at her brother and asked him if he remembered how they used to talk to the angels when they were young. His eyes widened as he remembered and smiled as he said he remembered. She asked him if he ever called on his guardian angel to help him now. She reminded him he was on his own now and should not rely on his parents to remind him to check his behavior. She told him she was worried about him. He was her brother and she wanted him to succeed. She advised him to start talking to his guardian angel every day and night. He said that was a good idea but he would never remember to do it. I will text you every morning and every night, she said. I really believe your life will change if you start taking positive steps to help yourself. He said he has doubts that anything would change. Why was I born with a temper and you were born so peaceful, he asked. She said she didn't know but maybe they were meant to compliment each other. Maybe I am here to help you find peace and you are here to teach me that not everyone is as calm as I am. Sometimes I don't understand how people exist when they are angry all the time, or when they are always negative about life, or even when they dislike themselves. So you are helping me understand a little about these personalities. I feel driven to reach out to you and these individuals and give them some of my inner peace. I know I have this inner calm but I don't know what I am supposed to do with it. Sometimes I feel guilty because I see others get frustrated and anxious, and difficult situations don't affect me that way. So in a way, I am like you. I have this personality that I feel I must extend to others and you have a personality you feel you must understand and temper.

They both went off to college after a summer of walks together delving into each other's psyche. They parted with tears because he loved to be around his little sister since she brought him total peace. The young girl loved meeting new people and developing friendships. She gravitated toward others with a similar peaceful personality. They supported each other helping the agitated and negative personalities around them. She gravitated toward psychology and criminal justice. She had seen many angry and agitated personalities at school get arrested for violent behavior. She recalled her brother's personality each time she read of these arrests in the school paper. She wanted to understand the 'why' of these personality traits and felt an inner pull to reach out and help them. She wanted to help them identify their agitated personalities and help them experience peace. She brought this to the attention of her friends who always reached out to help people. They had not thought of reaching out to these types of personalities. A few thought it a good idea but the majority was against it. They said it was dangerous. They warned her that these people were not stable and she could be harmed. She refused to think that way recalling her brother and some of his anger attacks. He needed help to understand his actions just as she believed these personalities on campus needed help to understand themselves and to experience peace maybe for the first time in their life.

As a senior in college with several psychology and criminal justice courses completed, the young girl established an organization for students who were having difficulty with their tempers. She insisted each counseling session, whether it was with a group or an individual, end with a guided meditation of peace. The campus organization was slow to be received. Many students were afraid they would be labeled as 'problem students' if they were seen going through the doors. However, when a few success stories emerged, the organization caught the attention of the college president. Faculty examined how college kids were helping fellow college kids. They were very impressed with what they observed. At graduation, the young girl received recognition and an award for her insight into the needs of troubled personalities. Her brother was very proud of her. He told her that he believed this was her reason to be on earth. She laughed and told him he was the reason for her to see that these personalities were inherently good people. I kept looking at you, she said, and I knew in your heart you were good. I could see you needed to be guided to truly see yourself and experience peace. I believed once you felt true peace, even for a second, you would want more and the more you got, the more you would want. So tell me, big brother, how did you come to this calm state I see now. I hope it is not drugs, she said. He laughed and told her he did try drugs. He wanted to escape himself. After being drugged up in his room for several days, he looked in the mirror and scared himself. He said he looked like death was not far away. Thoughts of you started to come into my head, he said, and then I remembered our conversation about the angels. I don't know why but I stared at this ugly face in the mirror and asked an angel to come to me. I didn't expect anything; the words just came out of my mouth. I think I was really scared and thought I would die right in front of the mirror. I struggled to clean myself up and then you came into my mind again. This time it was your peace I always felt when we were together. Sis, he said, I really believe you saved me. I am lucky to have you for my sister and for all the years we were together at home. I would like to be a part of your life helping others if you will have me. I promise, no temper tantrums, no violent outbursts. That is all behind me.

The young lady and her brother started small, as she did in college, to establish a center in their hometown to help young teens with disruptive personalities. Again, many of the children resisted her help. So, the young professional switched gears for these teenagers. She introduced them to a calm, non-threatening environment first. If any of them became disruptive, they were asked to leave immediately. Instead of walking them out the front door, the young director offered them a soda or cup of coffee. Their agitated bodies wanted to run at this point, but they lingered because they saw she was not reacting to their behavior. Most of them who reached this point stopped, looked at her, and flopped into a chair. The young director's brother would then walk in to help his sister. The young teens usually became alert seeing a male walk in, but relaxed when he flopped in a chair just as they did. She left these troubled teens with her brother who related to their behavior and anticipated their comments and resistance. Together the brother and sister developed a very successful program for angry, disruptive teens.

As the young girl and her brother progressed through life, she still did not feel completely satisfied with her work. She felt she was on the earth plane to do more. She talked to the angels daily for protection and guidance. She especially implored our help to show her another path in life to help distraught people. We were guiding her towards a path to help disabled individuals who were unable to accept their disabilities. The young girl was open to receiving our messages and signs. As she headed toward a physical therapy facility to establish her program, her eyes were drawn toward a building as she stopped for a red light. Surrounding this building were many street people, some of whom were in wheelchairs or leaning on canes. She went around the block to assess the situation again. We immediately sent her warning messages to get out of this area but she was being drawn in. She rationalized these people probably needed her more than the others. This was not the path she was supposed to be on. She felt our messages to leave the area but decided to park her car and talk to this group of disgruntled people. As she approached, several in the group alerted the others. They believed her to be with the authorities. Walking up to the group she immediately held out her hand and introduced herself as a therapist trained to help troubled and disabled people. Several of the older ones snickered and made some comments she could not understand. She still believed they needed help until she saw the person in the wheelchair stand up and walk away saying he didn't want any help from the authorities. She stared at him not from what she heard but from what she saw. He had no disability. She was shocked. Why was he impersonating a crippled person? Then, she heard another say he made a bundle on a corner in an upscale neighborhood. Suddenly, she realized she walked into a gang of thieves. She knew she was in danger. She quietly called to us angels for help. We sent messages for her to fill herself with calmness. She stood her ground on the corner with these people because she knew she would probably die if she ran. One in the group approached her and demanded money. She said 'no' very firmly. He was shocked because he never had that type of response to his demands. She heard that demand as she used to hear her brother demanding from her. She learned at an early age how to stand up and be strong against her brother. She instinctively used the same technique. Her eyes locked with his eyes. It was a standoff. She always won with her brother because his angry personality became frustrated with her strength and he would walk to his room and slam the door shut. However, she was on a street corner and there was no door to slam shut. As the man's frustration began to build with their eyes locked, he pulled a gun from his pocket. The rest of the group scattered with the sight of the gun. They were thieves not murderers. I appeared behind the man with the gun and loudly told him to put the gun on the ground. Of course, he thought it was the police and started to run but was blocked by two large dogs growling and ready to jump at my command. He turned quickly in my direction but I was already escorting the young lady to her car. The dogs kept him from retrieving his gun. When I returned to the angry man, he stared at my eyes. Who are you, he yelled. You don't look like the police because they would have handcuffed me by now. I just stared back at him and asked if he remembered talking to the angels when he was a little boy. He hollered, WHAT...are you telling me you are an angel? I just continued to look at him and told him to look into his heart to make that decision. I picked up the gun and asked if he wanted it back. He said no. The dogs and I walked away as the man stared after us shaking his head.

The young girl continued developing her program of helping angry people of all ages and in all walks of life, the rich, the poor, the disabled, the sick, the young, and the old. Her method of introducing them to peace and teaching them how to fill their hearts with peace to remove their anger grew in popularity across the world. She gladly accepted speaking engagements to share her program with millions of people. She worked closely with her brother until they were both well into their seventies. We were very proud of this soul as we watched her progress successfully through life on the earth plane. When she returned to us, she immediately recognized me as rescuing her from the man with the gun. She thanked me for coming to her rescue and allowing her to survive and spend the rest of her life on earth helping others. She successfully completed her written life plan. She beamed with happiness and ran to meet God when He entered to tell Him of her success. God smiled, held out his hands to her and lovingly said, 'congratulations and welcome back'.

When her brother returned to us, his earthly sister was there to welcome him back. She was very proud of him because he not only succeeded in his written plan but also advanced his soul even more than anticipated while on earth. His goal was to overcome a deep seeded anger in his soul. He returned to earth several times to dispel this anger but was never completely successful. This incarnation proved a success. After completing his written plan of ridding his soul of anger, he moved on to use his past experiences with anger to help others. It is a great honor for a soul to reach that level of being: to give totally of themselves to other souls who are struggling with their own life goals.

His guardian angels were ecstatic as they monitored his accomplishments. He hugged his earthly sister when he arrived with his guardian angels. He thanked her for her support and strength. He told her she was the main factor for his success. His angels then escorted him to God who was beaming with happiness. God lovingly hugged the spirit and whispered 'well done, my son, well done'.

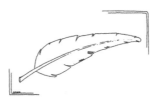

CPSIA information can be obtained
at www.ICGtesting.com
Printed in the USA
FFHW021805030119
50047970-54838FF